MW00608062

Native American Lesson Plans: A Look into Natives Today

A teacher's guide & lesson plans
Second Edition
For Grades K-12

By: Meredith Schramm
Illustrated by: Ruben Zendejas

Native American Lesson Plans: A look into Natives Today
Text Copyright: Meredith Schramm
Illustrations Copyright: Ruben Zendejas
Printed in Lehi, UT   2019
ISBN: 978-1-64633-145-1

Printed copies of assignments to be made for classroom purposes only.

To host a training with this book please contact: nativelessonplans@gmail.com

Table of Contents

1.
Introduction

The lessons provided in this book are meant as an aid and as an extra resource for your Native American unit. The new standards indicate that teachers are supposed to be teaching about how the Native culture has evolved today. However, this can be a difficult subject to research, and as a teacher, I know the last thing you want to do after a long day of teaching and grading is research and write more lesson plans. My hope is that by doing the research and writing, I can make it easier for you as a teacher to meet those standards.

Included in this lesson plan book are 14 lessons, with a unit project, assignments, and assessments. They are stand-alone lessons. If they fit your schedule, you can use all or just a few. They are meant to be an addition to what you are already teaching; a way to add a little more depth and a different perspective to the topics presented. This perspective is one that is greatly needed in this area of study to help change a false narrative that has persisted in education for so many years.

Most textbooks are written by non-Natives. As I was going through the current textbook for the 7th graders in my area I found that I was troubled by the focus of the textbook as it didn't address any of the relevant issues that faced Native Americans in history or that face Natives today. For example, In the textbook they define the word **tribe**. The word tribe is a vocabulary word they are required to learn in the 4th grade. However, the textbook defined it, and then moved on. It didn't talk about the different tribes, how many there were or are, or how each tribe is different. I also found that the textbook contained only a single paragraph about reservations, and that paragraph made reservations sound like a really great thing. It simply stated that the government gave them jobs, land, food, and money. The reality of the treaties and reservation system was a lot more nuanced. This whitewashed version of history really does students a disservice and felt dishonest to me. Most students reading the text would have made many incorrect assumptions.

Another reason the narrative needs to be changed is to gain a greater understanding of each other. There are so many examples in the news today of conflict between Natives and non-Natives. I honestly think that if people really understood each other's perspective, they would have a greater respect and compassion toward each other.

And lastly, our Native students feel invisible. We teach so much about the past that we forget to teach that Natives are still here. We are missing a great opportunity to teach about how Natives are living and impacting the world today. There are many amazing examples of current Natives that can give additional color and perspective to a lesson rather than focusing on what type of teepee or hogan a Native tribe lived in.

How to Use the Lessons
The lesson sections are meant to be informational. They give you as teachers background information, and information for discussion purposes. Obviously, when teaching to younger grades the information presented needs to be more basic, as opposed to teaching high school students. Tailor the lessons as needed to fit your students. In most lessons, there are multiple assignments, and each assignment has varying degree of difficulty. Please use your judgment on what would be best for your students.

There is also a book suggestion at the beginning of most of the lessons. I picked these books because they talk about and show Natives today. They are not legends of a long time ago, but talk about stories of little Native kids asking questions and dealing with present-day situations. If you can find them at your local library or online, I would highly suggest getting them. They are a good way to teach the lesson, and start a discussion with your students.

There is also an optional Unit Project. This project will help students focus on individual tribes, tribal issues, and topics today.

2.
Diversity Training: How can I better help my Native American students?

Diversity training. Is it really necessary? Can't we just treat all kids the same and call it good? In a perfect world, yes. But our world is far from perfect, and we know that kids come from all different backgrounds and stories. I will try to make this short, sweet, and as painless as possible. I want to give you a quick background on Native education, and ways you can help your students. However, each situation and family dynamic is different, just as all tribes and traditions are different. This is just a general guide.

Robert McGhee, Vice Chairman of the Poarch Band of Creek Indians Tribal Council, wrote in the 2016 State of Native Youth report: "...If you don't know where you come from, how can you know where you are going? With over 560 Tribes and Alaska Native villages, all possessing unique histories and cultural backgrounds, it is often difficult to determine one unified approach to overcome challenges and obstacles we face across Indian Country. But our sovereign nations possess one unique distinction that contributes to our resilience: *community*." ("Drawing Strength From Our Cultures")

Many of our Native youth come from communities that are affected by high poverty rates, unemployment, substance abuse, gang affiliations, and low educational attainment. Native youth also have a suicide rate that is two times the national average (Jiang, Caroline et al.). Despite the challenges they face today, having a strong ethnic identity and cultural affiliation have had a positive impact on our youth. The connection between culture, family, and their community makes a difference.

The Family Unit
The easiest way for me to describe the family dynamic is with the movie *My Big Fat Greek Wedding*. Pay attention to the way the extended family works in this movie. The family is big; there are cousins that are like siblings; the grandparents want their grandkids to know everything about their culture. Things need to be done a certain way within that culture, there is always food, and even the smallest occasion calls for an extended family gathering. Although the foods and traditions are different, many Native families come from a family with a similar dynamic. Family is important. Family members teach us about our culture and who we come from, our ancestors. Elders are respected and valued. We listen to them, and they help teach and direct us in how we carry on our traditions.

In my own family, and in working with Native families, I have noticed a common thread. Everyone works together to raise the kids. Aunties watch their nieces and nephews as their own, and cousins are valued like siblings. Kids may be shuffled between houses, and from the outside it may look a little chaotic, but it works.

Boarding Schools
I want to briefly discuss boarding schools because it will give you a little historical context around Native education. During the 19th and 20th centuries, entire generations of Native children were removed from their homes and forced to attend boarding schools. These schools compelled Native children to convert to Christianity and speak English. The schools forbade the practice of their cultural traditions and Native languages. Students' hair was cut and their tribal clothes destroyed. Sexual, physical, and emotional abuse in the schools were prevalent and thousands of Native children died due to beatings, medical neglect, and malnutrition. This formal policy of the United States government was referred to as "Kill the Indian, save the man." (American Indian Relief Council.)

When we think of the boarding schools era, we probably think it happened for a short period in the 1800s, but that is simply not true: Theodore Roosevelt Indian Boarding School, 1923–2016, now operates as a tribal school today. Riverside Indian School, 1871–present. St. Louis Industrial School, 1887–1949. Shawnee Boarding School, 1923–1961. This is just a small list of boarding schools that operated into more modern times. There were hundreds of boarding schools all across the United States. There are even Native boarding schools that still exist today.

However, most of the schools were closed by 1960. What does this mean? It means that my parents, and your students' grandparents, were alive during the boarding school era, and many attended boarding schools. Boarding schools were not usually a positive experience, and the boarding schools created a distrust of the school system that is still felt today by many Native families.

My father once made the comment that his generation was the first generation in a long time to live with their families full time. During the boarding school era, Native kids would only be home for the summers, and when they were home they would need to work or help watch the younger kids. School life and home life were separate. When my grandmother had kids who attended public schools, she was new to this type of schooling and didn't know what to expect or how to help her kids. My grandmother never had an example of helping kids with homework, or had ever even been taught the importance of education. Rather, education had a negative connotation similar to brainwashing. Like many things, this mentality can be passed on from generation to generation. However, the Native youth of this generation are stronger. They are paving the way for future generations to gain an education. They are doing this by adapting and drawing strength from their culture.

What Can You Do?

As teachers and educators, you are the main factor in helping build bridges and trust between Native families and the education system. The first thing you can do to help your Native students and families is to understand and respect their culture and religion. There are lots of stories in Native culture that have to do with the "Creator" or "Great Spirit." From these stories, we can see there is a spiritual aspect to Native culture. The culture and the religious or spiritual are very much intertwined. How would you want teachers to teach about or treat your religious affiliation?

For example, in the Jewish religion, many men wear a yarmulke for prayer purposes. However, when we teach about this, we would never have the kids make a yarmulke out of paper and send them home wearing it. It is disrespectful. The same goes for Native Americans. Eagle feathers are used for religious purposes. They are used as a form of prayer and for ceremonies. For these reasons, Native Americans are legally the only people who can possess eagle feathers. Out of respect for the culture and religion, we need to stop making paper feather headbands and fringe vests out of paper bags!

Second, it is okay to teach that the Europeans who came to America hundreds of years ago did not treat Natives well. There are a lot of positives that have come from the United States of America being created. However, it is okay to acknowledge that perhaps we didn't go about creating this free country the right way. The original colonists killed Natives and destroyed communities. Though Natives defended themselves, the colonists did great damage. How can we learn from our past if we don't fully understand it? Much of our history is a sad one. While we may not think our kids need to hear it, this history needs to be told. We need to empower our kids to be proud of who they are and their culture.

Third, let's think about doing away with Columbus Day celebrations. Many states and cities are moving toward Indigenous People's Day instead of Columbus Day. If you look at what really happened when Columbus came to the Americas, it was not a happy story. By celebrating Indigenous People's Day, we honor those people who originally inhabited our continent. For more information on the topic read the book, "Rethinking Columbus, the Next 500 Years" (Bigelow).

Fourth, teach about Native Americans today. There is no better way to help empower our Native youth than for them to feel proud about who they are and what their people have accomplished. I hope the lesson plans provided are a starting block to helping you teach about today's Natives.

Fifth, utilize your Native families. They want to share and teach, let them. This will also build trust. By reaching out, you will let them know you are invested in their kids, and want to teach their culture the correct way.

3.
Unit Plan

Standards: All lessons were created using the National Curriculum Standards for Social Studies put out by the National Council for the Social Studies. Lessons were also created using Common Core National Standards for Language Arts, Math, and Writing, as well as references to the Utah Core Social Studies Standards. Each lesson utilizes multiple standards for a deeper cross-curricular experience.

NCSS: Theme 1 - Culture
1. Human beings create, learn, share, and adapt to culture.
2. Cultures are dynamic and change over time
3. Through experience, observation, and reflection, students will identify elements of culture as well as similarities and differences among cultural groups across time and place.

NCSS: Theme 3 - People, Places, and Environment
1. The study of people, places, and environments enables us to understand the relationship between human populations and the physical world.
2. During their studies, learners develop an understanding of spatial perspectives, and examine changes in the relationship between peoples, places, and environments.
3. Today's social, cultural, economic, and civic issues demand that students apply knowledge, skills, and understandings as they address questions.

NCSS: Theme 5 - Individuals, Groups, and Institutions
1. Institutions are the formal and informal political, economic, and social organizations that help us carry out, organize, and manage our daily affairs.
2. It is important that students know how institutions are formed, what controls and influences them, how they control and influence individuals and culture, and how institutions can be maintained or changed.

NCSS: Theme 6 - Power, Authority, and Governance
1. The development of civic competence requires an understanding of the foundations of political thought, and the historical development of various structures of power, authority, and governance. It also requires knowledge of the evolving functions of these structures in contemporary U.S. society, as well as in other parts of the world.

CCSS: Writing
2. Write informative/explanatory texts to examine and convey complex ideas and information clearly and accurately through the effective selection, organization, and analysis of content.
7. Conduct short as well as more sustained research projects based on focused questions, demonstrating understanding of the subject under investigation.
8. Gather relevant information from multiple print and digital sources, assess the credibility and accuracy of each source, and integrate the information while avoiding plagiarism.

CCSS: Reading
1. Read closely to determine what the text says explicitly and to make logical inferences from it; cite specific textual evidence when writing or speaking to support conclusions drawn from the text.
3. Analyze how and why individuals, events, and ideas develop and interact over the course of a text.
9. Analyze how two or more texts address similar themes or topics in order to build knowledge or to compare the approaches the authors take.

CCSS: Listening & Speaking
1. Prepare for and participate effectively in a range of conversations and collaborations with diverse partners, building on others' ideas and expressing their own clearly and persuasively.
2. Integrate and evaluate information presented in diverse media and formats, including visually, quantitatively, and orally.
4. Present information, findings, and supporting evidence such that listeners can follow the line of reasoning and the organization, development, and style are appropriate to task, purpose, and audience.

CCSS: Mathematics
Measurement & Data
3. Represent and interpret data.

Mathematical Practices
1. Make sense of problems and persevere in solving them.
3. Construct viable arguments and critique the reasoning of others.

UCSS: Utah Social Studies
1: Students will understand how geography influences community location and development.
2: Students will understand cultural factors that shape a community.
3: Students will understand the principles of civic responsibility in classroom, community, and country.

Materials Needed: Copies of the activities provided in this book, as well as copies of the books listed in each lesson to enhance the lesson. There are also a few videos in some lessons that are available through PBS to enhance the lessons.
Grade Level: K-12, with emphasis for 4th and 7th grades
Time: 15 days, each lesson is approximately 45-60 minutes

Desired Outcomes

Learning Goals:
- I can explain how Native American history has impacted Native American and American lives today.
- I can demonstrate respect for the Native American culture and Native American people today.

Understandings: From the National Council for Social Studies:

The study of culture prepares students to ask and answer questions such as: What is culture? What roles does culture play in human and societal development? What are the common characteristics across cultures? How is unity developed within and among cultures? What is the role of diversity and how is it maintained within a culture? How do various aspects of culture such as belief systems, religious faith, or political ideals, influence other parts of a culture such as its institutions or literature, music, and art? How does culture change over time to accommodate different ideas, and beliefs? How does cultural diffusion occur within and across communities, regions, and nations?

The study of culture examines the socially transmitted beliefs, values, institutions, behaviors, traditions and way of life of a group of people; it also encompasses other cultural attributes and products, such as language, literature, music, arts and artifacts, and foods. Students come to understand that human cultures exhibit both similarities and differences, and they learn to see themselves both as individuals and as members of a particular culture that shares similarities with other cultural groups, but is also distinctive. In a multicultural, democratic society and globally connected world, students need to understand the multiple perspectives that derive from different cultural vantage points.

Young learners can explore concepts of likenesses and differences among cultural groups through school subjects such as language arts, mathematics, science, music, and art. They begin to identify the cultural basis for some celebrations and ways of life in their community and in examples from across the world. In the middle grades, students begin to explore and ask questions about the nature of various cultures, and the development of cultures across time and place. They learn to analyze specific aspects of culture, such as language and beliefs, and the influence of culture on human behavior. As students progress through high school, they can understand and use complex cultural concepts such as adaptation, assimilation, acculturation, diffusion, and dissonance that are drawn from anthropology, sociology, and other disciplines to explain how culture and cultural systems function.

Evidence of Learning

Performance Tasks
- Culminating Project based on lessons and individual tribes
- Based on standards, see individual lessons

Many of the lessons involve students writing, comparing and contrasting regional Native American culture and their own culture. Karin Hess' Cognitive Rigor Matrix was utilized in the creation of the lessons.

Success Criteria
- Project rubric
- See individual lessons

Learning Plan

Overview of Tribe Unit Project

Students will have the opportunity to research a tribe of their choosing or a regional tribe. Each lesson allows for research on how their chosen tribe was affected by the various topics and ends in a culminating display and presentation. As the teacher, you can decide to give time during class or utilize this project for homework. This project utilizes many standards and allows students to add depth to their learning. Below is a brief description of what students can do with each lesson on this project.

Lesson 3: Students will get assigned a tribe.

Lesson 4: What boarding schools did the children from your tribe get sent to? Show on a map where it was located, and where it was in relation to their reservation.

Lesson 5: Where is the tribe's reservation located, and where was their tribe originally located in relation to where their reservation is now? Make a map.

Lesson 6: What treaties did the tribe make with the U.S. government, and how did/does that impact the tribe?

Lesson 7: Research if there are any nearby schools with Native mascots or symbols and find articles for and against using the mascot. If students cannot find a local article or enough information, have them use a professional/college team in the area.

Lesson 8: Find an individual from that tribe who has made a difference or helped the Native community today. Or research the most recent living tribal chairman.

Lesson 9: Research an individual, living or dead, from the past who has made a difference in the community surrounding the tribe.

Lesson 10: Research and find the tribe's creation/origin story.

Lesson 11: Find a picture of a person at a powwow online (in any dance style they choose). Have students print and label each part of the regalia. Or, have student research the traditional regalia worn by their specific tribe today.

Lesson 12: Research how to say "Hello," "Goodbye," and "I love you" in the tribe's language.

Lesson 13: Write report/essay on how certain events/dates have affected Native lives today? Use timeline worksheet.

Project Rubric

Lesson Component	Met Expectations
Lesson 3: Tribal Assignment	I chose a tribe from the list or one my teacher assigned to me. This is the tribe I will use for the rest of the project.
Lesson 4: Boarding Schools	I located where my tribe's children were sent to boarding school. I located on a map where the boarding school was/is located and labeled it. I will use this map on my display and during my presentation.
Lesson 5: Reservations	Using the map from Lesson 4, I located where my tribe was originally from and where they are located now.
Lesson 6: Treaties	I researched what treaties were made with my tribe and wrote about how the treaties impacted theirs lives today. This will be part of my display and presentation.
Lesson 7: Mascots	I researched if any schools or national sports leagues use a Native mascot or symbol. I located an article about how people in my tribe feel about the school or sports team using the mascot. I located pictures and wrote about why members are for or against the use of the mascot for my display.

Lesson 8: Native Americans Today	I researched a living or recent individual from that tribe who has made a difference or helped the Native community today, or I researched who is the most recent living tribal chairman. I wrote about how they have contributed to society to add to my display, and located pictures to add to my display.
Lesson 9: Native Americans From the Past	I researched an individual from the past who has made a difference in my tribe's community. I wrote about how they have contributed to society to add to my display, and located pictures to add to my display.
Lesson 10: Creation/Origin	I researched my tribe's creation/origin story. I typed up the story to add to my display. I also found pictures to add to my display.
Lesson 11: Regalia	I found a picture of a person at a powwow dressed in regalia. I printed the picture and labeled the parts of the regalia for my display. I also researched my tribe's traditional regalia and added that information to my display.
Lesson 12: Language	I researched how to say "Hello," "Goodbye," and "I love you" in my tribe's language. I added these phrases to my display.
Lesson 13: Timeline	I wrote an essay to go with my display about how specific events affected Native lives today. I used the timeline worksheet to help me. I utilized appropriate writing skills to finish the essay.
Presentation and Display	My display is neat, organized, and everyone can read it. I have proper citations for my research. have used correct spelling and grammar on my display. I have used the map(s) and pictures in a way that makes my board interesting to look at. I have been thoughtful and respectful of the tribe I have researched as I put my display and presentation together. I presented my information clearly. I made eye contact with my audience members. I knew my information well enough that I only used my board as a reference during the presentation.

Unit Progression

Week	Monday	Tuesday	Wednesday	Thursday	Friday
Week 1	Who Are Native Americans? Pre Assessment	What is Culture?/ Thanksgiving Lesson *(Hand out debate worksheet in preparation for the mascot lesson.)*	Differences in Tribes, Clans	Boarding Schools	Boarding Schools, *Unspoken*
Week 2	Reservations/ Sovereign Nations	Treaties/DAPL & Bears Ears	Mascots	Influential Native Americans Today	Code Talkers
Week 3	Storytelling/Creation	Dance & Regalia	Drumming & Song	Doctrine of Discovery	Post Assessment

Note: Lessons can be taught individually. However, the depth of student tasks and unit plan was built for all lessons to be completed and taught.

4.
Lessons 1 & 14: Native Americans Today - Pre/Post Assessment

Lesson: Pre Assessment
Standards:
NCSS: Theme 1
NCSS: Theme 2
CCSS: Reading
1. Read closely to determine what the text says explicitly and to make logical inferences from it; cite specific textual evidence when writing or speaking to support conclusions drawn from the text.
3. Analyze how and why individuals, events, and ideas develop and interact over the course of a text.

Materials: Copies of timeline
Time: 30-60 minutes, depending on the grade

Desired Outcomes

Learning Goals:
• I can identify different factors that have shaped Native American culture today.

Understandings:	**Essential Questions:**
Students will understand that Native culture extends past what is talked about in history books. Natives are still around today. Over the next few weeks, they will learn about significant events that have shaped Native American culture.	What do you know about Native culture today? What do we know about who Native people are and their traditions? What are current issues in Native country? And who are some influential people in Native culture?
Students will know… (Knowledge & Vocab)	**Students will be able to… (Skills):**
For this unit, we will learn about Native Americans in the past, and that Native Americans still live today. We will learn that Native Americans live just like us, and live in homes and drive cars. We will learn that even though Native Americans live just like everyone else, they hold on to their culture and still follow some of their traditions today.	• Utilize writing skills • Utilize research skills • Apply information learned to another tribe/situation

Evidence of Learning

Performance Tasks:	**Success Criteria:**
• Timeline worksheet, or • What is Native color page	• I filled in the timeline sheet with the events that impacted Native American culture. • I am able to write or explain how the events shaped Native American culture today. • I know where I need to focus my learning of Native American studies. • I can explain why I colored the Native American color page the way I did.

Learning Plan

Lesson:

Tell the students that today they are starting their Native American unit. For the next few weeks, the class will be talking about Native Americans in the past, and present, and how the Native American culture has changed over time to what it is today.

Before going into much detail, pass out a copy of the timeline that goes along with this lesson. Explain their assignment. You will give them a few minutes to fill out the timeline. If they don't know it, then leave it blank. This sheet will stay with them through all of the lessons. As you teach about the different events, students can fill it in. This timeline will be a part of their big project due at the end of the unit.

You may begin by finding out what the class knows about culture today. What do they know about who the people are and their traditions?

As you go through the lessons, you can reinforce the significant events that have shaped the current Native culture. For this unit, the students will learn about Native Americans in the past, and will also learn that Native Americans still live today. The students will learn that Native Americans live just like us, and live in homes and drive cars. They will learn that even though Native Americans live just like everyone else, they embrace their culture, and still follow many of their ancient traditions.

Discuss: "Do any of you know anything about what is going on with Native Americans today?" "What are issues or current events they are dealing with?" "Who are influential Native Americans in the community?"

Read the following:

> "To understand the present, it is important to have a deep awareness and understanding of the past. Specific to the history and formation of this country, we must collectively move to a position of greater knowledge regarding the role and significance of indigenous people within that history. Unfortunately, indigenous people are most often minimized to a brief existence and role within the context of history. However, the reality is that indigenous peoples played a tremendous role in the history of our country.'

> Prior to the European invasion, indigenous peoples flourished across this land—the woodlands tribes of the northeast, the plains tribes of the Midwest, the desert tribes of the southwest, the wetland tribes of the southeast, and the Pacific tribes of the northwest. As this nation was born and expanded, the result was the decimation and genocide of a people and their way of life. The depth and magnitude of this decimation is often absent from the pages of history. The resulting displacement of a people and their struggle to find a new identity is often absent from the pages of history. The result has been a lack of adequate awareness and understanding by most people about their own country's indigenous people.

> While our numbers have diminished post-European contact, we are still here today. We are proud people with our own traditions, customs, stories, and beliefs. We are proud people who often walk between two worlds. We are proud sovereign nations working to empower our people and build communities. We are the living and breathing indigenous people of this land. We are not romanticized people you see in movies and books. We are not caricatures you see portrayed in cartoons and as mascots. We are not historical footnotes.

> As this nation continues to grow, it must be honest with its past. Indigenous people must be lifted from the objectified existence that people too often place them within. To fully understand and appreciate who we are today as a country, we must recognize all that was sacrificed and lost. As a country, we must

acknowledge the history and relationship with the indigenous people and indigenous nations of this land. This is an appropriate expression of respect; not the respect supposedly expressed and made evident in such manifestations as the Washington Redskin, the Atlanta Brave, or the Cleveland Indian. Respect is not found within books that refer to indigenous peoples as savages, wild, or reckless. Respect for indigenous people comes in the form of reconciling the past with honesty and acknowledging the present.

We are the proud people of the sovereign nations within this country. We are an educated people. We are a people rich in culture and traditions. We are a self-determining people with governance and structure working to ensure a positive future for our people. We are a people who have suffered, but who more importantly have chosen to preserve and endure. We are the indigenous people of this land." (E. Zendejas vii) -Kitcki Avery Carroll, Cheyenne & Arapaho Tribe of Oklahoma, University of Nebraska at Omaha/Class of 1998

After reading this excerpt, tell the students that, while we will be learning about the history of Native Americans, we cannot fully understand the history without learning about the present.

Adaptations for younger grades:
Tell the students that today they are starting their Native American unit. For the next few weeks, we will be talking about Native Americans in the past and present. Before going into too much detail, pass out the color page of the two kids (page 14). Tell the students that we are going to pretend that we have a new student coming to our class tomorrow. All we know is that he/she is Native American, or "Indian."

Have them color what they think our new student will look like on the handout given. Then give the kids a few minutes to work. Time's up! Have students put their colors away.

Discussion time: Invite a few students to show and share what they drew. Some of the kids may have drawn feathers on their head, or drawn buckskin on their clothes.

After a few kids have shared, ask the class what else they know about Native Americans and write their answers on the board. Answers will probably include things like: They have powwows, live in teepees, hunt buffalo, or wear feathers.

While these are all true answers, tell them a lot of what we know about Native Americans comes from what we see in books, on TV, or in movies. For this unit, we will learn about Native Americans in the past, which includes when Native Americans lived in teepees and hunted buffalo, but we will also learn that Native Americans still live today. And we will learn that Native Americans live just like us, and live in homes and drive cars. We will learn that even though Native Americans live just like everyone else, they may still follow some of their traditions today.

Assignments:
Timeline: The timeline worksheet is to be used as a study guide to help them throughout the unit. As they learn about the different dates and policies, have the students write them down. The timeline will also be a requirement for their end of unit poster board.

Timeline Answers:

1860 - Bureau of Indian Affairs established the first Indian Boarding School.

1887 - General Allotment Act, also known as The Dawes Act, authorized the President to divide land for individual Indians.

1924 - Indian Citizenship Act conferred U.S. citizenship on all Native Americans.

1934 - Indian Reorganization Act restored tribal lands and permitted tribes to reorganize under federal law for purposes of self-government.

1945–1968 - Termination Era was when the U.S. government tried to force Natives to assimilate and terminated tribes.

1968 - Indian Civil Rights Act applied most of the Bill of Rights' requirements and guarantees to Indian tribal governments.

1975 - The Indian Self-Determination and Education Act reaffirmed Congressional policy that tribal governments should be permitted to control education programs, contracts, and grants affecting Indians.

1978 - American Indian Religious Freedoms Act was the policy that allowed Natives to preserve their traditional religious rights.

1978 - Indian Child Welfare Act (ICWA) established federal rules ensure that Indian children removed from their homes are placed with Indian families whenever possible to preserve cultural values.

1993 - Indian Tribal Justice Act gave the responsibility of the U.S. government to tribal governments, including protection of the sovereignty of each tribal government.

Timeline

1860 - First Indian Boarding School:

1887 - General Allotment Act:

1924 - Indian Citizenship Act:

1934 - Indian Reorganization Act:

1945-1968 - Termination Era:

1968 - Indian Civil Rights Act:

1975 - Indian Self-Determination and Education Act:

1978 - American Indian Religious Freedoms Act:

1978 - Indian Child Welfare Act (ICWA):

1993 - Indian Tribal Justice Act:

Imagine we had a new student in our class, and I told you he or she was Native American. What do you think he would look like? Use the pictures of the kids below as an outline, and color!

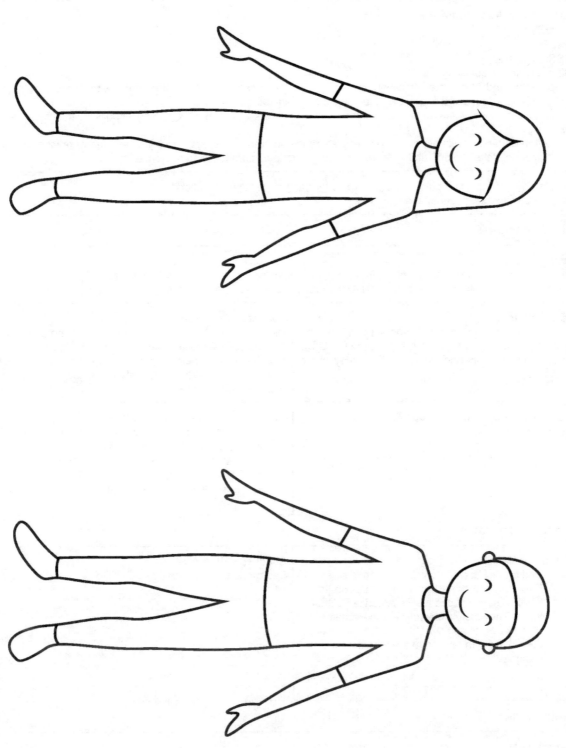

Lesson 14: POST ASSESSMENT

Lesson: Post Assessment
Standards:
NCSS: Theme 1
NCSSS: Theme 2
CCSS: Listening & Speaking
1. Prepare for and participate effectively in a range of conversations and collaborations with diverse partners, building on others' ideas and expressing their own clearly and persuasively.
2. Integrate and evaluate information presented in diverse media and formats, including visually, quantitatively, and orally.
4. Present information, findings, and supporting evidence such that listeners can follow the line of reasoning and the organization, development, and style are appropriate to task, purpose, and audience.

Materials: Timer for student presentations. Rubric for each student/presentation.
Time: 30 - 60 minutes, depending on grade.

Desired Outcomes

Learning Goals:
- I can explain how Native American history has impacted Native American lives today.
- I can demonstrate respect for the Native American culture and Native American people today.

Understandings:	**Essential Questions:**
Students will show a greater understanding of the significant events and people that have shaped Native American culture, specific to the tribe they were researching.	Did the students complete all of the required pieces of the project? Were the students prepared when it was their turn? Was their work neat, and done to the best of their ability? Were the students able to show understanding of their topic?
Students will know… (Knowledge & Vocab)	**Students will be able to… (Skills)**
See rubric for unit project.	<ul><li>Present and speak clearly</li><li>Utilize writing skills</li><li>Utilize research skills</li><li>Utilize reading skills</li><li>Apply information learned to another tribe/situation</li></ul>

Evidence of Learning

Performance Tasks:	**Success Criteria:**
<ul><li>Unit project board and presentation to class.</li><li>Essay on how the events and policies on the timeline have shaped Native American culture today. They should also include examples of current events and people from the information they found with relation to the tribe they were assigned.</li></ul>	See rubric for unit project.

Learning Plan

Lesson: Student presentations.
As you have been teaching the lessons, students should have been completing the mini assignments and questions that went along with each lesson. They should have had time to complete a poster and a written essay to present and read to the class. Each student will be given a few minutes to present. Make sure students include all of the information on the rubric.

5.

Lesson 2: The Thanksgiving Lesson

A note from the author:

During the month of November, we celebrate Native American Heritage Month. November also happens to be the month where America celebrates Thanksgiving. This is typically a month where we teach about the first Thanksgiving: pilgrims and Indians. It is a time where teachers tell students about how both the Indians and pilgrims sat together and had a big feast. I have been to schools where half of the class were Indians dressed in paper feathers and paper bag vests, and the other half of the class were pilgrims adorned with pilgrim hats made out of paper. There are a few things that are wrong with this lesson. First, the facts and history we are teaching are romanticized. I recently attended a conference in Connecticut where the tribes in the area, including the Wampanoag, discussed their version of the 'Thanksgiving Story.' Many explorers had landed on the eastern shores many times. The tribes in the area simply ignored them and they did their own thing. However, in 1620 when the pilgrims landed, they had women and children with them. Women and children are honored and respected in the culture, and the Wampanoag knew they wouldn't survive without their help. So we read about how the Natives in the area taught the pilgrims how to live off of the land. However, Thanksgiving for them is seen as a day of mourning. It was the day, or event that changed their life. In their eyes, after the first feast, the pilgrims took over their land, gave them illnesses, and after much fighting, pushed them onto reservations.   Second, as we will explore further in the Dance and Regalia lesson, feathers are a sacred symbol for Native Americans, even today, and should not be used in our lessons.

I know it is easy and fun, and many teachers think it's okay because it's what has traditionally been done. But I am asking teachers to *please stop*! For the Thanksgiving Day lesson, let's turn the focus off of the traditional "Pilgrims and Indians" narrative and more toward gratitude. Teaching about Native Americans during the month of November is still a good idea. However, the lessons should be honest, and not a whitewashed story with a happy ending. They should celebrate Native American heritage and culture and embrace the good and the bad. Take the time to look through this book and find a lesson plan that will fit with your curriculum to incorporate into your teaching during November, or you can use the following lesson to replace the traditional Thanksgiving Day lesson.

Lesson: The Thanksgiving Lesson
Standards:
NCCS: Theme 1
CCSS: Reading
1. Read closely to determine what the text says explicitly and to make logical inferences from it; cite specific textual evidence when writing or speaking to support conclusions drawn from the text.
2. Determine central ideas or themes of a text and analyze their development; summarize the key supporting details and ideas.
3. Analyze how and why individuals, events, and ideas develop and interact over the course of a text.
Utah Standards:
Objective 2: Explain how selected indigenous cultures of the Americas have changed over time. Identify how indigenous people maintain cultural traditions today.

Materials Needed: Culture Tree color page, copied. Crayons, pencils. Paper plate, glue, scissors.
Time: 30-60 minutes, depending on grade level and time given for students to write their essay

---

Desired Outcomes

Learning Goals:
- I can explain what about my culture I am grateful for.
- I can explain the similarities and differences between my culture and a regional Native American culture (based on where you live).

Understandings:	Essential Questions:
Student will understand what culture is, why culture is	What is culture? What cultural group do I belong to?

important, and similarities and differences between the student's culture and a regional Native American culture (based on where you live).	What traditions do I celebrate, and what food do I eat that are from my culture? What are the similarities and differences between the regional Native American culture and my own? Why am I grateful for my culture?
Students will know… (Knowledge & Vocab) Culture is arts, food, celebrations, and traditions based on your surroundings or ethnic groups. Culture helps us understand who we are and where we come from. It also helps us understand traditions that have come from our culture.	**Students will be able to… (Skills)** • Compare and contrast • Writing skills

Evidence of Learning

Performance Tasks • Culture Tree • Compare and contrast cultures • Narrative essay on the topic "I am grateful for my culture." • Narrative essay on the topic "My 1620."	**Success Criteria** • List one food, art, celebration, and tradition from my culture. • List one food, art, celebration, and tradition from a regional Native American culture. • Utilize writing traits and rubrics for the essay.

Learning Plan

What is culture? **Culture** is art, culture is food, culture is celebrations. Culture includes traditions we do with our families and community. Lots of traditions are centered around holidays. Culture is a way to express ourselves and our identities.

Examples:

Culture: American
Art: Theater, Museums
Food: Hotdogs, Hamburgers
Celebrations: Birthdays, Halloween

Culture: Native American (Navajo/Diné)
Art: Sand Paintings
Food: Blue corn mush
Celebrations: Navajo Weddings, Powwows

Culture: Chinese
Art: Calligraphy
Food: Dumplings
Celebrations: Chinese New Year

Culture Tree: In the trunk of the tree, have the student write down one of their own cultures.
In the leaves labeled 1, 2, and 3, have the students write down three things that represent that culture, using what they learned in class. Culture is art, food, and celebrations. Complete the second tree for the regional Native American culture.

Compare & Contrast: Using a Venn Diagram, have the students compare and contrast their culture and a regional Native American culture. Once students have listed the similarities and differences they will be able to move on to writing their essay.

Essay on the Topic: "I am grateful for my culture.": Have students write an essay explaining why they are grateful for their culture, what traditions their family has, what their family does for Thanksgiving, and what they have learned about the regional Native American culture. Depending on the grade level, students can do more research and cite evidence. They can also go deeper with how culture changes over time and is shaping our society today.

Essay prompt: "What is my 1620?" As we read in the editor's note at the beginning of the lesson we learn that the Thanksgiving feast was an important event that impacted the Wampanoag tribe. What event in your life is your 1620? What event, good or bad, has made an impact on your life. How have you overcome your challenges?

My Culture

Name: _____ Date: _____

Name: _____ Date: _____

1.

2.

3.

Cultures

6.

Lesson 3: Differences in Tribes, Clans

Lesson: Differences in Tribes & Clans **Standards:** NCSS: Theme 3 (See unit plan) CCSS: Reading 1. Read closely to determine what the text says explicitly and to make logical inferences from it; cite specific textual evidence when writing or speaking to support conclusions drawn from the text. 2. Determine central ideas or themes of a text and analyze their development; summarize the key supporting details and ideas. 3. Analyze how and why individuals, events, and ideas develop and interact over the course of a text. 4.RI.3 Explain events, procedures, ideas, or concepts in a historical, scientific, or technical text, including what happened and why, based on specific information in the text. 4.MD.B.4 Make a line plot to display a data set of measurements in fractions of a unit (1/2, 1/4, 1/8).
Materials Needed: *Teachers, the lesson gives you a lot of information that you can read over and discuss with your students. A lot of the policies and treaties are important for understanding other lessons in the unit.* If you are able to find a map of the current tribes and where they are located, it would be a good visual. You will also need copies of the activities located at the end of the lesson. **Time:** 30-60 minutes, depending on grade level and time given for students to research the regional Native American tribes

Desired Outcomes

Learning Goals: • I can explain what the New Deal was in 1934, and how it has impacted Native American tribes today. • I can explain how tribes determine membership in my region and can graph the different blood quantums. • I can explain the concept of clans as family units within tribes.

Understandings:	**Essential Questions:**
Students will understand that, before 1934, the United States government policy on Native Americans was to try and assimilate them to become more "American." By 1934, the U.S. tried to reverse the traditional goal of assimilation by giving tribes ownership of reservations, lands, and minerals. The U.S. government used the Indian Reorganization Act of 1934, also known as the Indian New Deal to help rectify the previous policies. The Bureau of Indian Affairs (BIA) set up a series of standards for tribes to prove they were tribes so they could take ownership of said lands. Students will also understand how each tribe is set up differently. With the New Deal, tribes were allowed to set up their own form of government and control membership within the tribe. Students will understand, each tribe member is also part of a clan, or family grouping. Each tribe sets up their clans differently and clans are still used to determine relationships within tribes.	How many federally recognized tribes are in the United states? What does it mean to be federally recognized? What was the Indian New Deal? What are the three different criteria tribes use to decide membership within the tribe? What are clans?

Students will know... (Knowledge & Vocab)	**Students will be able to... (Skills)**
What it means for tribes to be federally recognized, and the criteria that need to be met by the BIA (Bureau of Indian Affairs). Students will understand what the Indian Reorganization Act of 1934 is, and how it affected	• Utilize writing skills • Utilize research skills • Utilize graphing skills • Utilize reading skills

Native tribes. Students will understand what it means to assimilate, and why the United States government felt it necessary. Students will also understand what clans are and the different roles clans play in tribes.

Evidence of Learning

Performance Tasks
- Word search
- Q&A worksheet
- Informational graph

Unit Project Assignment
Students will be assigned a tribe to research. You can use the list of tribes on the Tribal Word Search sheet, or you can find tribes more local to your region.

Success Criteria
- I am able to list many tribes that are federally recognized in the United States.
- I am able to explain the criteria for tribes becoming federally recognized.
- I am able to explain the guidelines for membership for different tribes in my region.

Learning Plan

Tribes:

In the United States, according to the Bureau of Indian Affairs, there are 573 federally recognized tribes (as of 2018). Of those, 229 tribes are located in Alaska, while the rest are located in 33 other states. (National Congress of American Indians 15) (Many of the states without tribes are located on the east coast where Natives were either pushed west or perished.)

In order to be federally recognized by the Bureau of Indian Affairs, each tribe has to meet 7 criteria. (Federal Recognition Services by American Ancestors)
1. The tribe has been identified as an American Indian entity on a substantially continuous basis since 1900.
2. A predominant portion of the tribe comprises a distinct community and has existed as a community from historical times until the present.
3. The tribe has maintained political influence or authority over its members as an autonomous entity from historical times until the present.
4. The tribe must provide a copy of its present governing documents and membership criteria.
5. The tribe's members consist of individuals who descend from a historical Indian tribe or tribes, which combined and functioned as a single autonomous political entity.
6. The membership of the tribe is composed principally of persons who are not members of any acknowledged North American Indian Tribe.
7. Neither the tribe nor its members are the subject of congressional legislation that has expressly terminated or forbidden recognition.

These criteria are mainly for new tribes trying to get federally recognized. When the U.S. government was putting tribes on reservations and organizing tribal status, there were many tribes during the 1934 Indian Reorganization Act that did not get tribal status. These criteria are still relevant today, as many tribes are still working on becoming federally recognized by the federal government. Essentially, what these 7 criteria are proving is that each tribe has its own government and laws, its own language, traditions, and history. They need to prove that they existed as a tribe before 1900. This is a process that can take years, and has taken many tribes decades to prove. Over time, as more tribes achieve federal recognition, the number of tribes has gone up.

Since 1978 the Bureau of Indian Affairs (BIA) have been forcing Natives to prove their existence through this federal recognition process. Currently there are still about 220 tribes that are categorized as 'unrecognized.' Of those 220 tribes, about 100 of them have already signed treaties with the federal government, but they were not ratified by the U.S. government. (Manatake American Indian Council)

Indian Reorganization Act of 1934:This was the federal legislation that dealt with the status of Native Americans, often called the Indian New Deal. Previously, the government stance on Native Americans was "Kill the Indian, save the man." They wanted to force Natives to be "white Americans" or to assimilate. **Assimilate** means to take on information, ideas, or culture; to resemble or liken. They did this by taking away land, and forcing Native children to attend boarding schools where they were not allowed to speak their language or practice many of their traditions.

By 1934, the federal government wanted to reverse the traditional goal of assimilation. Tribes were given ownership of reservations, land, and minerals. Tribes became federally recognized, establishing governing bodies within the tribes. Prior to 1934, Native Americans were not usually allowed off reservations without permission from the U.S. government.

However, in 1953 the United States Department of the Interior (DOI) began implementing the termination phase of the Act, following clauses that had been added by congress. This was also known as the Termination Era. Again, Native Americans were dealing with the fact that the Federal Government wanted to try and assimilate them. It was a means for Congress to end all relations between the tribes and the federal government. The House Concurrent Resolution 108 of 1953 was the beginning of the official termination policy. This resolution caused the immediate withdrawal of all federal aid, services, and protection, as well as reservations from the various tribes. The termination of tribes had the biggest impact on education, health and tribal economies. Due to this forced assimilation and combined with the Native's lack of knowledge (taxes, industry, healthcare system, business, law, etc.) and the high unemployment rates, most of the Native population fell into poverty. (American Indian Movement)

After seeing the economic downfall of many Native populations after their tribal recognitions were terminated, the government finally passed a law in 1968 called the Indian Civil Rights Act. This applied most of the Bill of Rights' requirements and guarantees to Indian tribal governments. In 1975 the Indian Self-Determination and Education Act was passed which reaffirmed Congressional policy that tribal governments should be permitted to control education programs, contracts, and grants affecting Indians. Slowly tribes were able to regain their tribal status through the federal recognition process.

As of 2018, there are now 573 federally recognized tribes in the United States. One of the latest being the Pamunkey Indian Tribe in Virginia. The Pamunkey Tribe became federally recognized in 2016 and is the first tribe recognized in the state of Virginia.

Each tribe is different. In order to be recognized as a tribe, they had to prove that they were a separate organization or group from any other tribe. Most tribes have their own language. All tribes have an origin story, or a story on how they believe their people came to this earth. Each tribe has their own governing body that allows them to govern their people and manage their land. They are allowed to control who can be enrolled in the tribe or not.

Each tribe has their own set of rules or guidelines to allow membership in the tribe. Most tribes will use one of three criteria to establish membership (E. Zendejas 38-39):
1. **Blood Quantum**: Tribes will require a person to be a certain amount of "full-blood" Native to be enrolled in the tribe. Usually, tribes will require a person to be at least 1/4, but there are some tribes who require as little as 1/16 or as high as 1/2 degree of blood.
2. **Lineal Descent:** Some tribes require a person to be of lineal descent or of blood relationship to a historical member in order to be enrolled in the tribe.
3. **Adoption:** Most tribes will allow an adoption process. However, adoptions are mainly for ceremonial purposes.

Clans:

All tribes, even today, are comprised of clans. **Clans** are family groups within a tribe. This can be compared to having a family last name. Typically your whole family has the same last name. It helps identify you as a family. What helps set them apart as a family unit is their clan. When they introduce themselves to someone new, their clan name is always included with their name. And in many tribes, the different clans had their own purpose or responsibility within the tribe. One clan would be responsible for hunting/gathering. One clan would be responsible for farming, etc. Everyone in the tribe had their job, and they worked together as a community.

Clans still exist today. If you are enrolled in a tribe, you most likely know what clan you belong to. There are no specific roles or jobs associated with clans today but they do help Natives keep track of who belongs to what family. When formally introducing themselves, Natives will often include what clan they belong to.

What do we call people who are Native American? The terms Native American, American Indian, or Indian are all correct, and most will not be offended by any of these terms. But because each tribe is so different, many Natives find they most like to be identified by their tribal name. For example, "I am Navajo." instead of, "I am Native American."

Assignments:

- Unit Project: Talk about the unit project and what is expected. Pass out rubric as well as assign tribes to each student.
- Word Search: There are currently 573 federally recognized tribes in the United States. The word find only lists a few of them. Find their names in the word search.
- Q&A Worksheet: Students can fill this in as you teach the lesson as interactive notes or it can be used after the information is presented.
- Informational Graph: Have each student or group of students research your region's Native American tribes to find out what criteria each tribe uses for membership. (Related to question 7 on the Q&A worksheet). Once they have this information, have them create an informational graph about your region, such as a bar graph, pie chart, pictograph, or line plot (based on your grade level standards).
- Discussion/Group Project: Pick a tribe and have students research and figure out what information they need to prove the 7 steps for their tribe to be federally recognized.

Adaptations for younger grades:

Policies and federal regulation may be a little too much for younger kids to take in, but you may focus on a few points for the younger kids to understand:

1. There are 573 different Native American tribes in the United States today (this does not include Canada).
2. In 1934, the United States government made a set of guidelines that each tribe had to meet in order to be a tribe. This meant that each tribe had to have its own language, its own stories, and its own government in order to be called a tribe.
3. Many tribes are similar because of where they lived. But each tribe is different.
4. In order to be a member of a tribe, each person has to prove they are a descendent by blood or by proving they are related to a historical member of the tribe.
5. Clans are family groups in each tribe. Each tribe has different clans, and the clan's purpose is different in each tribe.
6. Today people use their clans as a way of showing they are related.

Tribal Word Search

Name: _____ Date: _____

There are currently 573 federally recognized tribes in the United States. Below is a list of just a few of them. Use the list below to find them in the word search.

Yaqui	Yavapai	Hopi	Paiute
Apache	Navajo	Pomo	Tejon
Wiyot	Nez Perce	Seminole	Mashantucket Pequot
Shoshone	Kickapoo	Wampanoag	Assiniboine
Sioux	Crow	Blackfeet	Cheyenne
Omaha	Winnebago	Ute	Pueblo
Oneida	Cherokee	Osage	Ottawa
Ponca	Oglala	Goshute	HoChunk
Tulalip	Yupik	Athabaskan	Sac and Fox

```
M A S H A N T U C K E T P E Q U O T C H O C K N W
S H O S H O N E H I Z U U T K C H E Y E N N E E A
O M O K S N X R Q U P L S A G A W J O T T M B Z M
X F X I L P O T L C L A W I N O B O N E I D A P P
A S S P E R C P O M O L W A N P H N Z E M I P E A
T I L U U E Q A N M M I B L A C K F E E T E A R N
G O T Y A Q U I B E A P Y A I P K L P M N E C C O
O S A G E U X U B L H W A P U E B L O A M I H E A
G G P Q V X N T I O A W O C H E R O K E E V E R G
A R I T H U T E E N A H J Q W L I K I C K A P O O
B F A A U O L I N I Y N A P O O L K A Y N M O L S
E T P W B I H Z X M T H V I N H O C H U N K L L H
N D A A H S H K Y E I L A M N H N L W O S W V X U
N R V T O E I N A S S I N I B O I N E B O S O X T
I P A T H A B A S K A N N Y P B R U J R K F N C E
W I Y O T O O G L A L A C S S K S A C A N D F O X
```

Tribe & Clans - Fill in the Blank

Name: _____ Date: _____

1. There are _____ federally recognized tribes in the United States.

2. In order to be federally recognized by the BIA (Bureau of Indian Affairs), each tribe has to meet 7 criteria.

      a.

      b.

      c.

      d.

      e.

      f.

      g.

3. The Indian Reorganization Act of 1934 is also known by what name?

4. What is the name of the first tribe to be recognized in the state of Virginia?

5. List three different criteria tribes use for membership:

      a.

      b.

      c.

6. Describe what clans are within a tribe?

7. Research a regional Native American tribe in your area. What criteria do they use to recognize membership?

7.

Lesson 4: Boarding Schools

Lesson: Boarding Schools **Standards:** NCSS: Theme 2 NCSS: Theme 5 NCSS: Theme 6 CCSS: Reading 1. Read closely to determine what the text says explicitly and to make logical inferences from it; cite specific textual evidence when writing or speaking to support conclusions drawn from the text. 2. Determine central ideas or themes of a text and analyze their development; summarize the key supporting details and ideas. 3. Analyze how and why individuals, events, and ideas develop and interact over the course of a text. 9. Analyze how two or more texts address similar themes or topics in order to build knowledge or to compare the approaches the authors take. CCSS: 4.RI.5 Describe the overall structure (e.g., chronology, comparison, cause/effect, problem/solution) of events, ideas, concepts, or information in a text or part of a text. CCSS: 4.RI.6 Compare and contrast a firsthand and secondhand account of the same event or topic; describe the differences in focus and the information provided.

Materials: Activities located at the end of the lesson. Optional: *Unspoken: America's Native American Boarding Schools* (DVD) **Suggested Books:** <ul><li>Littlefield, Holly. *Children of the Indian Boarding Schools.* Summary: This book is a factual book about the life and history of Indian boarding schools. The information spans from the creation of boarding schools to the present, with a lot of pictures.</li><li>Bunting, Eve. *Cheyenne Again.* Summary: In the late 1880s, a Cheyenne boy named Young Bull is taken to a boarding school to learn the white man's ways.</li><li>Sheinkin, Steve. *Undefeated: Jim Thorpe and the Carlisle Indian School Football Team.* Summary: This book is about the life of Jim Thorpe and his rise to be one of the greatest athletes of all time. However, the book gives a greater understanding of when Jim was at boarding school, and it also talks about why the boarding school was started. This book is 233 pages, but an easy read for young readers.</li><li>Jordan-Fenton, Christy & Pokiak-Fenton, Margaret. *When I was Eight.* Summary: An Inuit girls experience as she first enters boarding school.</li><li>Jordan-Fenton, Christy & Pokiak-Fenton. *Not My Girl.* Summary: The second book to *When I was Eight, My Girl* is the girls experiences when she returns back to the reservation. She has to relearn her families teachings and way of life.</li><li>**Time:** 30-60 minutes, depending on grade level and time given for students to research and write their essay</li></ul>

Desired Outcomes

Learning Goals: <ul><li>I can explain why boarding schools were created and how they were influential in Native American history.</li><li>I can explain several causes and effects relating to the boarding school era.</li></ul>

Understandings:	**Essential Questions:**
Students will understand the reasoning behind the boarding school system, why it was wrong, and what the government tried to do to fix what happened. The students will also be able to compare and contrast a typical day at a boarding school and a typical day at a public school. And how the Indian Child Welfare Act (ICWA) is used to best protect the interests of Native children.	What was the reasoning behind sending young Native children to boarding schools? What was life like at a boarding school? What hardships did children have to face while at boarding schools? What would children do during the summer when there was no school? What was the law passed in response to Native children being taken from their homes?

27

Students will know… (Knowledge & Vocab)	Students will be able to… (Skills)
Assimilate means to take on ideas or a culture. The Indian boarding schools were meant as a way to assimilate children to becoming more "American." Students will also know of the "placing out system," where students were sent to work during the summer to better the skills/trade they learned while in school. The Indian Child Welfare Act (ICWA) of 1978 was passed to help stop the high number of Indian children being taken from homes. ICWA transferred power back to the tribes.	• Compare and contrast • Utilize writing skills • Utilize research skills • Utilize reading skills • Apply information learned to another tribe/situation

Evidence of Learning

Performance Tasks	Success Criteria
• Compare and contrast Venn diagram of the student's first day of school with boarding school • Research and write an essay on the Indian Child Welfare Act (ICWA) **Unit Project Assignment:** What boarding schools did the children from your tribe get sent to? And show on a map where the boarding school was located in relation to their reservation.	• I will be able to name one thing that is different from my school experience and a boarding school experience. • I will also be able to name one thing that has changed from the boarding school experience to more recent approaches to Native education. • I can list three things that ICWA does for Native people.

Learning Plan

Lesson:

School for Native Americans today is a lot different today than in the past. Today, Native American children attend public schools, just like you and every other child. It has taken a long time for education to be what it is for Native children.

In 1860 that the Bureau of Indian Affairs (BIA) opened the first boarding school for Native American children.

Boarding schools are not like schools today. Native children were taken from their homes and families and sent to live at special schools called boarding schools. There, they would learn to assimilate. **Assimilate** means to take on ideas or a culture. The government thought at the time that if Native children were sent to boarding schools, and were taught English and forced to learn the "American way of life," that Natives could be civilized. One phrase that was used to describe this belief was the idea that boarding schools would help the government to "Kill the Indian, save the man." The government thought that if they took away their culture, their languages, and their beliefs that the Natives would live and be a part of the "American Culture" (National Museum of the American Indian). Essentially, the government did not want them to be Native anymore. They wanted to take away their culture.

Native kids in boarding schools were not allowed to speak their own language, and were also not allowed to practice any religious ceremonies. Even though pilgrims came to America to escape religious persecution; Native Americans were not granted this same religious freedom until 1978 when the American Indian Religious Freedoms Act was passed. This policy allowed Natives to preserve their traditional religious rights. During this time, students were taught Christianity. Students were also taught math, reading, science, and even art (National Museum of the American Indian).

A typical day at a boarding school was spent doing regular course work like reading, math, and history. And the other half of the day was spent teaching trades. Girls were taught to cook, sew, and clean. The boys learned skills that required manual labor such as farming or shoemaking (MNOpedia).

To the outside world it looked like the United States was doing a good thing. The Native children were given an education, food, and skills. But to a little Native child, it was anything but good. Families and community were and are at the heart of Native American beliefs and way of life. It was a sad day when the children were separated from their parents. If a family refused to send their children to the schools, agents on the reservations would withhold food rations, or in some cases they had officers that would forcibly take them.

Because schools were so overcrowded, and students lived in tight spaces, sickness and disease spread like wildfire. Many children died from those diseases, and from malnutrition.

A few of the schools had a system called "placing out system," which placed the Native children in the mainstream community for the summer to "better learn their skills." Girls were put in white homes for domestic labor for families, and boys were put in seasonal harvest or unwanted jobs by immigrants. It was not a happy life, or a life they were used to (American Indian Relief Council).

By the 1880s, there were 60 schools in operation with over 6,200 students. By the early 1900s, there were hundreds of Indian boarding schools all over the country. There are still a few off-reservation boarding schools that are in operation today, but since funding has declined, so have the schools. By 1960, about 80 percent of the boarding schools had closed (American Indian Relief Council).

In 1978, Congress passed the Indian Child Welfare Act (ICWA). This law was passed in response to an alarmingly high number of Native children being removed from their homes by both public and private agencies. ICWA set federal standards that apply to state custody proceedings involving an Indian child who is a member of, or eligible for membership in a federally recognized tribe. ICWA allowed the transfer of Indian child welfare cases back to tribes. The stated purpose of ICWA is "To protect the best interests of Indian children and to promote the stability and security of Indian tribes and families by the establishment of minimal Federal standards for the removal of Indian children from their families" (U.S. Department of the Interior Indian Affairs).

With ICWA, the states could no longer force children from their homes to attend boarding schools. By the time ICWA was passed, it was estimated that hundreds of thousands of Native children had gone through the boarding schools. Do boarding schools still exist today? Yes, there are a few schools still in operation (U.S. Department of the Interior Indian Affairs).

- *Unspoken: America's Native American Boarding Schools* is a good documentary to watch. You can find it on kued.org. It is approximately 57 mins. Direct link to video https://tinyurl.com/y9433x2e.

Teachers can also read the following testimonials of someone who created a boarding school and his reasoning, and one student who attended the boarding school. Teachers can also use the documentary *Unspoken* to contrast more students experiences in the boarding school system who attended more recently.

Captain Richard Henry Pratt: Testimonial taken from *Undefeated: Jim Thorpe and the Carlisle Indian School Football Team.*
The Carlisle Indian Industrial School was Richard Henry Pratt's creation, his life's work. After fighting in the Union Army during the Civil War, Captain Pratt had gone west in the late 1860s to serve in the U.S. government's wars against Native Americans. The government had already forced Native Americans from east of the Mississippi River—including the Potawatomi and Sac and Fox ancestors of Jim Thorpe—onto reservations; now it was doing

the same to the nations of the West. Pratt was part of the effort—he was an Indian fighter, with no regrets. "I had concluded," he'd later confess, "that as an army officer I was there to deal with atrocious aborigines."

In a series of ferocious wars, the U.S. troops removed nearly all the Native American nations of the West from their lands, forcing thousands of people to resettle on reservations. At the same time, railroad crews were hammering tracks across the West, farmers were stringing barbed wire around the most fertile land, and government was paying hunters to wipe out the once-vast buffalo herds Plains Indians had depended on for food.

All of this resulted in what newspapers called the "Indian Problem." Native Americans could no longer live in their traditional ways; they didn't have access to the land or resources anymore. Yet they were not part of the thriving economy of the West, either. Stuck on isolated chunks of land settlers didn't want, they lived far from cities and industries and jobs. Indian families couldn't produce enough food in the lousy reservation soil—but if they left the reservation to hunt on land that had always been theirs, they were treated like outlaws, arrested, or even shot.

So what next? That was the problem. Richard Henry Pratt had helped create it. He also believed he had the solution. In the ten years in the West, Pratt's views had gradually changed. Working alongside Cherokee and Choctaw allies, guarding Comanche and Cheyenne prisoners of war, Pratt got to know many of them as individuals, as human beings. He'd come to see that, despite cultural differences, there was no difference between Indians and whites in terms of intelligence or ability. If Indians could no longer live in their traditional ways, Pratt decided, they should be taken into white American society instead.

Pratt's answer to the "Indian problem" was to treat Native Americans as if they were immigrants to the United States. His answer was to help young Indians—if necessary, to force them—to assimilate into white American culture.

The way to accomplish this, he reasoned, was with a boarding school in the East. The school would be far from the reservations of the West, so students would be cut off completely from their families and traditions. Pratt's plan was harsh, and he didn't try to sugarcoat it. "I believe in immersing the Indians in our civilization," he declared "and when we get them under, holding them there until they are thoroughly soaked."

To put it bluntly, Pratt did not respect Indian culture. He seems to have genuinely believed he was helping the people, but he began with the bigoted conviction that white American civilization was superior to all others. The rich diversity of Native American cultures and languages, the complex relationships between nations, the thousands of years' worth of knowledge about living in this part of the world—Pratt dismissed it all as savage and worthless.

"Left in the surroundings of savagery, he grows to possess a savage langage, superstition, and life," Pratt would say of Indian children. "All the Indians there is in the race should be dead," he said. "Kill the Indian in him, and save the man."

Pratt approached the government with his idea for an Indian School. He was given permission to use Carlisle Barracks, an abandoned military base in central Pennsylvania. The next step was to somehow persuade Native American parents to trust him with their sons and daughters. In the fall of 1879, Pratt set out for the Rosebud Reservation, a Lakota reservation in the dry, hilly prairies of the Dakota Territory (Sheinkin 26-29).

Life at Carlisle Indian School: Taken from *Undefeated: Jim Thorpe and the Carlisle Indian School Football Team.* Pratt's plan was to strip these kids of their Indian identities, and he started right away. He took away their moccasins, blankets, and deer-hide leggings. Girls were given long gray dresses and heavy stockings. Boys were handed wool suits, itchy red long underwear, and farmer's boots. Students marched into classrooms and sat at wooden desks. One student, Ota Kte, recalled a white woman—the teacher, he figured—was standing in front of a chalkboard, writing what appeared to be a series of meaningless squiggles. "Do you see all these marks on the blackboard?" the teacher asked her class through an interpreter. "Well, each word is a white man's name. They are going to give each one of you one of these names by which you will hereafter be known."

The teacher motioned for a boy to come to the front of the room. She handed him a long wooden stick and gestured for him to point to one of the clumps of squiggles. There were names from the Bible, names of U.S. presidents, though, of course the students had no way of knowing this. Besides, these children already had names, names rich in meaning, names given to them to honor relatives or to recognize special traits or achievements.

The boy turned to the class, looking for guidance. Finally, he pointed randomly to one of the names. The teacher wrote the name on a piece of white fabric and sewed it to his shirt. Then she erased that name from the blackboard and called on another student. When it was Ota Kte's turn, he pointed to a name that turned out to be "Luther." From that point on, he was known as Luther Standing Bear.

Next came the haircuts. Lakota boys traditionally wore their hair in a long braid—Pratt considered this "uncivilized." One by one, the boys were called out of class and led to a room where a barber had set up his chair and tools. The barber cut off each boy's braid, then cropped his hair close. Like many of the boys, Ota Kte felt tears fill his eyes as his hair fell to the floor.

But most days at Carlisle were routine—strict, grinding, boring routine. Pratt ran his school as a military academy, with every minute of the day accounted for. A bugler woke students at five-thirty, and they marched to exercise before breakfast. At meals, they sat on long benches in the dining hall while school staff watched over them, correcting table manners. Students spent most of the morning in the classroom, learning reading, writing, history, and math. Afternoons were for vocational training. The boys learned carpentry, tailoring, printing, baking; girls practiced cooking, canning, sewing, child care.

Pratt watched it all. From his favorite spot on the bandstand in the middle of campus, he inspected the student's clothes, their hair, the polish on their shoes. He lectured them and urged them on (Sheinkin 32-40).

Adaptations for younger grades:
Read *Cheyenne Again*, or another book that is listed in the suggested books at the beginning of this lesson plan.

Focus on the reasons why students were told to go to boarding schools, and what a typical day would look like.

How did you feel on your first day of school? How would you feel if you were told you had to attend a boarding school?

Assignments:
- Compare and contrast what students have learned about Native boarding schools to the school they attend now. How is it similar? How is it different?
- ICWA (Indian Child Welfare Act) is still a huge part of Indian policy today. It covers much more than just placement of Indian children. Have students learn and research ICWA and write a paper on their findings.

Compare and Contrast

Name: _____ Date: _____

After learning about Native American boarding schools, compare and contrast the difference between your school experience and the boarding school experience.

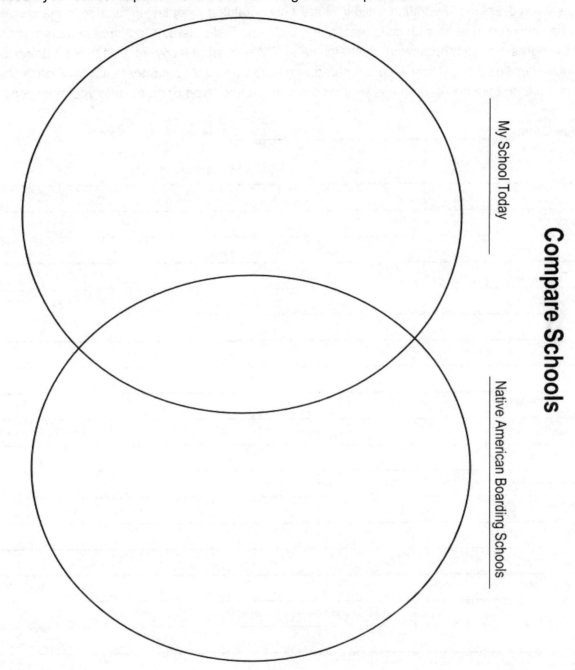

My School Today

Native American Boarding Schools

Compare Schools

Name: _____ Date: _____

Indian Child Welfare Act

Research & Essay: The Indian Child Welfare Act contains a lot of law in relation to the welfare of Indian children. It deals with child placement, including foster care, adoption, and parental and tribal rights. For your homework, research what ICWA is, what it covers, and how it relates to Native families today. Then write a 5 paragraph essay on your summary of ICWA. Please use this sheet to take notes, then use your own paper to either type or hand write your final copy.

Due Date: _____

_____

_____

_____

_____

_____

_____

_____

_____

_____

_____

_____

_____

_____

_____

_____

_____

_____

_____

_____

_____

_____

8.

Lesson 5: Reservations/Sovereign Nations

Lesson: Reservations/Sovereign Nations
Standards: NCSS: Theme 5 NCSS Theme 6 CCSS: Writing 3. Write narratives to develop real or imagined experiences or events using effective technique, well-chosen details, and well-structured event sequences. UCSS: Objective 1: Describe the responsibilities and rights of individuals in a representative government as well as in the school and community. d. Explain how the influence and power of individuals is affected when they organize into groups.
Materials: Copies of worksheets. **Time: Time:** 30-60 minutes, depending on grade level

Desired Outcomes
Learning Goals: • I can explain the impact the Iroquois Confederation made on making the United States government. • I can apply what I learned to ruling my own land.

Understandings:	**Essential Questions:**
Students will understand the importance of the Iroquois Confederation and how their government influenced the U.S. constitution. Students will also know that when the U.S. government signed treaties with the tribes, they were signing treaties as a sovereign nation. At the time, tribes were not considered part of the United States, and Natives were not legally American citizens. Each tribe was given land to live on, called a reservation. Students will also understand many important dates and how they affected Native Americans.	What was the Iroquois Confederation? How did the Iroquois Confederation influence the U.S. constitution as we know it today? What are treaties? How did the US government go back on the treaties made with the Native tribes?
Students will know... (Knowledge & Vocab)	**Students will be able to... (Skills)**
Sovereignty is the ability of a nation to govern itself. Tribes were sovereign nations. Treaties signed with the U.S. government allowed tribes to keep their sovereignty, not gain it. Assimilate means to take on ideas or culture. Reservations are lands set aside for each tribe to live on.	• Utilize reading comprehension skills • Utilize listening, recall, and application skills • Utilize writing skills • Utilize research skills • Apply information learned to another tribe/situation

Evidence of Learning
Performance Tasks / **Success Criteria**

Performance Tasks	**Success Criteria**
• Essay and questions • Worksheet **Unit Project Assignment:** Where is the tribe's reservation located? Make a map. Students can use the same map from Lesson 7. Show where the tribe was originally located in relation to where the reservation is now.	• I am able to define sovereignty, reservations, and assimilate. • I am able to explain the importance of the dates: 1831, 1945–1968, 1975, 1978, 1988, 1993. • I am able to name the six nations of the Iroquois Confederacy.

Learning Plan

Lesson:

Tribal governments are some of the oldest governments in the Western Hemisphere. Think about this concept for a moment. When the colonists came over from England, the form of government they were most familiar with was a monarchy. Part of the reason they wanted to come to America was to get away from that type of rule and government. However, Native governments were based on principles of equality, freedom, and respect. Right away, the founding fathers knew that the tribal governments were something to be emulated. By watching the tribal councils, the founding fathers observed that each representative spoke individually and everyone listened without interruption. Thomas Jefferson soon realized this was a more civilized way to conduct meetings, as opposed to what they were used to, where everyone had to yell in order to be heard.

Did you know that even the United States Constitution was modeled after the oldest constitution in North America? The Great Law of Peace, was the constitution that was created and used by an alliance of Indian tribes 400 years before the first settlers arrived (Iroquois Confederacy Constitution).

The Great Law of Peace is the oral constitution of the Iroquois Confederacy. The "Six Nations" of the confederacy are the Mohawk, Onondaga, Oneida, Cayuga, Seneca, and the Tuscarora people. The original five members ratified this constitution near the area of Victor, New York. The Tuscarora Nation was added later in 1722. The laws were first recorded by way of wampum symbols and later translated into English. The Great Law of Peace is a set of laws that are divided into 117 articles and outline the role of government and leadership within the nations. The six Iroquois nations are symbolized by an Eastern White Pine Tree, called the Tree of Peace (Iroquois Confederacy Constitution).

"I am Dekanawidah and with the Five Nations' Confederate Lords I plant the Tree of Great Peace. I plant it in your territory, Adodarhoh, and the Onondaga Nation, in the territory of you who are Firekeepers.

I name the tree the Tree of the Great Long Leaves. Under the shade of this Tree the Great Peace we spread the soft white feathery down of the globe thistle as seats for you, Adodarhoh, and your cousin Lords.

We place you upon those seats, spread soft with the feathery down of the globe thistle, there beneath the Shade of the spreading branches of the Tree of Peace. There shall you sit and watch the Council Fire of the Confederacy of the Five Nations, and all the affairs of the Five Nations shall be transacted at this place before you, Adodarhoh, and your cousin Lords, by the Confederate Lords of the Five Nations."
-Taken from the Constitution of the Iroquois Nations, The Great Law of Peace.

The Founding Fathers recognized tribal governments, and pledged that their sovereignty was to be protected (Tribal Sovereignty: History and Law).

Indian tribes were living on the land far before colonists started arriving. They were their own nations, and provided for and governed themselves. So when the tribes would sign treaties with the U.S., they were guaranteeing the right to continue governing for themselves. Meaning the sovereign rights they already had were to be retained, not granted. In 1831, the U.S. Supreme Court recognized tribal sovereignty in a court decision in *Cherokee Nation v. Georgia*. This court ruling stated that Indian Nations had the full legal right to manage their own affairs, govern themselves internally, and engage in legal and political relationships with the federal government.

Through much of the 19th century, a lot of federal policy changed toward tribes. Much of this had to do with the U.S. government wanting tribes to assimilate (*See lesson on boarding schools*). Then, the U.S. government made a major policy change starting in 1945 which marked the start of what we know as the Termination Era.

The years between 1945 and 1968 were known as the **Termination Period**. The United States government decided that federal recognition and assistance to more than 100 tribes should be terminated. The termination of federal assistance was an economic disaster for many tribes (see page 40 - *Tribal Lands* for more information). The federal government wanting Native Americans to become more civilized was nothing new. With the termination of tribes, there was an urgency among Native Americans to preserve what culture they had left. During this time frame, a movement was created by Native Americans called AIM, the American Indian Movement. The AIM was a series of protests by Native Americans to try and take back their land and they culture they felt was taken from them. Since the termination period, 78 of the 113 tribes that were terminated have been reorganized again (National Congress of American Indians 3).

Since the end of the Termination Era, there have been many policy changes that are important to Native government policies:

1968 - **The Indian Civil Rights Act:** This applies most of the Bill of Rights' requirements and guarantees to Indian tribal governments.

1975 - **Indian Self-Determination and Education Act:** Reaffirmed Congressional policy that tribal governments should be permitted to control education programs, contracts, and grants affecting Indians.

1978 - **Indian Child Welfare Act (ICWA):** Established federal rules to ensure that Indian children removed from their homes are placed with Indian families whenever possible to preserve cultural values.

1993 - **Indian Tribal Justice Act:** Gave the responsibility of the U.S. government to tribal governments, including protection of the sovereignty of each tribal government.

Today, tribal governments still exist for the same purpose as they were originally founded—to provide for the welfare of the Native people. Tribal governments continue to build and maintain services like water, roads, emergency assistance, law enforcement, and transportation. Tribal leaders look out for the well-being of their people in protecting their rights. They also work toward preserving and encouraging culture and supporting higher education (Tribal Sovereignty: History and Law).

Adaptations for younger grades:
Policies and federal regulation may be a little too much for younger kids to take in. But maybe focus on a few points for the younger kids to understand:
1. Native governments were based on principles of equality, freedom, and respect. Right away, the founding fathers knew that the tribal governments were something to be emulated. By watching the councils, the founding fathers observed that each representative spoke individually and everyone listened without interruption.
2. The United States Constitution was modeled after the oldest constitution in North America. The Great Law of Peace was the constitution that was created and used by an alliance of Indian tribes 400 years before the first settlers arrived.
3. Indian tribes were living on the land far before colonists started arriving. They were their own nations, and provided for and governed themselves. When tribes would sign treaties with the U.S., they were guaranteeing the right to continue governing for themselves. Meaning the sovereign rights they already had were to be retained, not granted.

4. Through much of the 19th century, a lot of federal policy changed toward tribes. Much of this had to do with the U.S. government wanting tribes to assimilate.

5. Today, tribal governments still exist for the same purpose as they were originally founded—to provide for the welfare of the Native people. Tribal governments continue to build and maintain services like water, roads, emergency assistance, law enforcement, and transportation. Tribal leaders look out for the well-being of their people in protecting their rights. They also work toward preserving and encouraging culture and supporting higher education.

Assignments:
- To learn more about tribal lands, have students read "Tribal Lands," then have them answer the questions: Answers: 1-Varies, 2-B, 3-A, 4-Varies, 5-More than 100
- Tribal Government & Policy: Students can fill the worksheet out as you teach, or you can have them fill it out at home.
- Writing Assignment: You suddenly wake up in a land where you are the ruler of the land. What kind of laws and policies would you put into place and why? Would any of them be similar to the Native American policies you learned about? Why?

Tribal Government & Policy

Name: _____ Date: _____

Define the following terms:
1. Sovereignty:

2. Assimilate:

3. Reservation:

Explain the importance and impact of the difference policies passed by the U.S. government:
1. 1831, Cherokee Nation v. Georgia:

2. 1945–1968 - Termination Era:

3. 1968 - The Indian Civil Rights Act:

4. 1975 - Indian Self-Determination and Education Act:

5. 1978 - Indian Child Welfare Act (ICWA):

6. 1988 - Gaming Regulatory Act:

7. 1993 - Indian Tribal Justice Act:

8. List the six nations of the Iroquois Confederacy and the importance of the Great Law of Peace:

Name: _____ Date: _____

Reading Comprehension - Tribal Lands

Read the following paragraphs on tribal land and reservations, then answer the questions.

Between the years 1828 and 1887 there was a lot of pressure by the United States government to move west. As the U.S. population grew, so did the military and military strength. This resulted in a forced migration of Native American tribes. The military used aggressive military force throughout the west to relocate tribes onto reservations. These reservation lands were established through treaties, or an agreement between two or more nations. The treaties were such that if Native Americans gave up a large amount of their land, they could continue the right of self-governance under the protection of the United States.

As more and more settlers were moving west and wanting more land, the United States government passed the General Allotment Act of 1887, also known as the Dawes Act. This gave individual Indians small parcels of land for ownership. Once the land was handed out, the surplus, or extra land, was taken by the government and sold to the settlers moving west. Nearly two-thirds of the land from the Allotment Act was taken from Native American tribes. During this time, Native Americans were not allowed to leave the reservation without permission. Leaving could result in arrest, and sometimes even death.

The years between 1945 and 1968 were known as the Termination Period. The United States government decided that federal recognition and assistance to more than 100 tribes should be terminated. The termination of federal assistance was an economic disaster for many tribes. The federal government wanting Native Americans to become more civilized was nothing new. As part of the plan, the government promised tribal members housing, and jobs in big cities if they moved off the reservation. Essentially, their intent was to encourage the abandonment of the reservations to make it easier to terminate the tribes. But most of those people who were promised housing and jobs were not given what was promised. With the termination of tribes, there was an urgency among Native Americans to preserve what culture they had left. During this time frame, a movement was created by Native Americans called A.I.M., the American Indian Movement. The A.I.M. was a series of protests by Native Americans to try and take back their land and culture that was taken from them. Since the termination period, 78 of the 113 tribes terminated have been reorganized again.

Today Native Americans are still trying to heal and rebuild. They have taken big strides to restore their communities to what they once were. Native American tribes are still fighting against the federal government over policies, treaties, and land. And they are still trying to find their identity. They are still trying to be heard. They are still here.

1. Why were Native Americans forced onto reservations? Use text evidence to support your answer.

2. What is a treaty?
    a. A term used to take away lands from Native Americans.
    b. An agreement between two or more nations.
    c. An after school snack.

3. The General Allotment Act was established to benefit which group of individuals?
    a. The federal government
    b. The U.S. population
    c. Native American tribes

4. Are Native American tribes still dealing with unfair treatment today? Give reasons for your answer from the text.

5. How many tribes were terminated between the years 1945 and 1968? Use text evidence to explain your answer.

Name: _____ Date: _____

Natives in the News

Native Americans still exist today. Your assignment will be to make an effort to look for different Native American issues or people in the news. Use any media outlet that you have available. Once you find an article, print it off or cut it out. Fill out the information, and then write a one page summary of the article. Bring this sheet along with the printed article to class.

The topic of an article you are to look for is on **'Tribal Reservation Land.'**

Title of Article:
Written By:
Media Source:
Date:
Tribe Affected:

Summary:_____

_____

_____

_____

_____

_____

_____

_____

_____

_____

_____

_____

_____

_____

_____

_____

_____

9.
Lesson 6: Treaties/Dakota Access Pipeline & Bears Ears

Lesson: Treaties/Dakota Access Pipeline & Bears Ears	

Standards:
NCSS: Theme 5
NCSS: Theme 6
CCSS: Writing
7. Conduct short as well as more sustained research projects based on focused questions, demonstrating understanding of the subject under investigation.
8. Gather relevant information from multiple print and digital sources, assess the credibility and accuracy of each source, and integrate the information while avoiding plagiarism.
9. Draw evidence from literary or informational texts to support analysis, reflection, and research.

Materials: Printed assignments
Time: 45-60 minutes

Desired Outcomes

Learning Goals:
- I can explain the meaning of treaties and how those treaties affect Natives today.

Understandings:	**Essential Questions:**
Students will understand that the reason the U.S. government made treaties with the tribes was because they were not granting rights, but guaranteeing the right to continue governing themselves, since they were already independent nations. Native peoples have a special relationship with the land and resources, and want to preserve and respect the land their creator gave them. Tribes are also fighting to keep the land that was honored to them in treaties. It is a battle that they are still fighting today.	What are treaties? Why did the U.S. government need to make treaties with the different Indian nations? How are those treaties affecting tribes today? What treaties were made that affected the land on Standing Rock Reservation and at Bears Ears National Monument? Why is it important for Native tribes to preserve their land?

Students will know… (Knowledge & Vocab)	**Students will be able to… (Skills)**
Treaties: Treaties are agreements between countries. **Dakota Access Pipeline:** A 1,172-mile-long oil pipeline is being built to carry crude oil from North Dakota to Illinois. **Bears Ears:** Bears Ears National Monument is a 2 million acre cultural landscape in southeast Utah that is considered sacred by numerous regional tribes.	- Utilize reading comprehension skills - Utilize listening, recall, and application skills - Utilize writing skills - Utilize research skills - Apply information learned to another tribe/situation - Apply knowledge to a presentation

Evidence of Learning

Performance Tasks	**Success Criteria**
- Discussion/presentation - Writing assignment - Optional article assignment - Research current news article **Unit Project Assignment:** What treaties were made between the tribe and the U.S. government? How did they impact the tribe?	- I was able to utilize the skill of writing to write my essay. - My essay is at least one page, 5 paragraphs. An introduction and conclusion paragraph with 3 supporting paragraphs. - I was able to apply the information gained from the article to my presentation.

Learning Plan

Lesson:

What are treaties? Treaties are agreements between countries.

Why did the U.S. government need to make treaties with the different Indian nations? The U.S. government needed to make treaties with the Indian tribes because the tribes were and still are sovereign nations. Indian tribes were living on the land far before colonists started arriving. They were their own nations, and provided for and governed themselves. So when tribes signed treaties with the U.S., they were guaranteeing their right to continue governing for themselves. The sovereign rights they already had were to be retained, not granted. In 1831, the U.S. Supreme Court recognized tribal sovereignty in a court decision in *Cherokee Nation v. Georgia*. This court ruling stated that Indian Nations had the full legal right to manage their own affairs, govern themselves internally, and engage in legal and political relationships with the federal government (*See lesson on Reservations/Sovereign Nations*).

For many years, treaties between Indian nations and the U.S. government were established to create borders and set out the standards of behavior between parties. The signing of the treaties ended in a mutual agreement between the two nations. Refer back to the lesson on Sovereign Nations and Reservations. If you read the essay on tribal lands, you learned that the U.S. government passed the General Allotment Act of 1887. The U.S. government had given lands, or reservations, to Native tribes in a series of treaties. Many of those treaties were broken in 1887 when the U.S. government took back more land.

So how does any of this affect Native tribes today? Native communities are still fighting the U.S. government to take back what was theirs. This best examples of this are on the Standing Rock Sioux Reservation and Bears Ears National Monument.

Standing Rock Sioux Reservation: A 1,172-mile-long oil pipeline is being built to carry crude oil from North Dakota to Illinois. Along that route it will cross the Missouri River. The Missouri River is the main water source for the reservations in the surrounding area. It will also cross 38 miles of sacred lands belonging to the Standing Rock Sioux tribe which was given to them in a 1851 treaty signed at Fort Laramie in Wyoming.

In July 2016, attorneys for the Standing Rock Sioux Tribe took their first legal action to block the pipeline from being built. Shortly after those legal actions were taken, hundreds of Natives from over 100 tribes came together to protest the pipeline. All around the campground there are signs posting "Mni Wiconi," which means "Water is Life." Why is water so sacred? Faith Spotted Eagle, a member of the tribe, stated in an interview done with CNN, "Water is the 'first medicine;' it sustains us in our mother's womb. It's used in ceremonies to heal people. The steam it gives off in a sweat lodge, for example, purifies. Water can clean a spirit when it's bleeding. It can calm a person and restore balance. Its power goes even deeper, though. Water has memory. When people speak or sing to it during a ceremony, it is believed that the water holds on to what it hears and can later share what it learns. So when a group of women gathers on the river's bank next to the crowded main camp and they hold up tobacco offerings while singing prayers, the water is listening" (Ravits).

The land that the pipeline is said to cross is on a burial ground. The tribe believes that if you disturb the land where their ancestors are buried then they will not have a clear path to the after world, and they will be stuck roaming this world (Ravits).

Bears Ears: Bears Ears National Monument is a 2 million acre cultural landscape in southeast Utah that is considered sacred by numerous regional tribes. Bears Ears is named for a distinctive pair of buttes said to resemble the crown of a bear rising out of the earth. Bears Ears is America's most significant unprotected cultural landscape. For the tribes of the Four Corners region (Ute Mountain Ute, Uintah Ouray Ute, Navajo, Hopi, and Zuni), Bears Ears is a sacred place where the spirits of the ancestors still dwell. Medicinal plants grow only in this area, and important ceremonies are performed here. Because of its diverse terrain, local Ute and Navajo people depend on this area for firewood collection and subsistence hunting. Bears Ears was also the birthplace of Navajo hero Chief Manuelito, making this an area of special significance. Together the five tribes are calling in a unified voice for the protection of the region (Utah Diné Bikéyah).

What is happening with Bears Ears Monument? A non-profit group called Diné Bikéyah, which means "People's sacred lands" in Navajo, is trying to preserve those sacred lands. This proposal marks the first time in history that Native American tribes have called upon the President of the United States to use the 1906 Antiquities Act to protect ancestral land. The five sovereign tribal nations are trying to work directly with the government and federal government. The plan of Bears Ears is set out to be a co-management of the monument, in which tribes will directly oversee management of the lands. The 8 member Bears Ears Commission will be comprised of one representative from each of the 5 tribes as well as a representative from each of three federal agencies that currently administer lands within the proposed monument boundary (National Forest, BLM, and National Parks). This will ensure that the land is used in ways that are consistent with Native values and traditions forever (Utah Diné Bikéyah).

The fight for Natives to preserve their land is still happening all over the U.S. The consequences of what happened long ago are still affecting Native tribes today. We may not notice it much in the news, but it is there. They are still trying to preserve their land, and preserve their culture.

- *Battle Over Bears Ears* is a good documentary to watch. You can find it on kued.org. It is approximately 57 mins. Direct link to video: **https://www.kued.org/whatson/kued-productions/battle-over-bears-ears.**

Assignments:
Take the time to have students look up and discuss/present:
1. What is currently happening with the Dakota Access Pipeline and Bears Ears? Discuss how it is affecting Native tribes in the area.
2. Discuss whether students think Natives have a right to protest how the land is being used.
3. Discuss how the situation would make them feel if it was affecting them?

Writing Assignment: Building upon the writing assignment in Lesson 8, students are ruling their own land and discover another group of people. The people are the only ones with access to a specific resource necessary to survive. How would you approach the other group of people? What kind of treaties would you try to put in place? Would any of them be similar to the treaties the U.S. government signed with the Native Americans? Why or why not?

Prior to the lesson, ask the students to bring in an article about the pipeline that they have read, and can discuss in class.

Name: _____ Date: _____

Natives in the News

Native Americans still exist today. Your assignment will be to make an effort to look for different Native American issues or people in the news. Use any media outlet that you have available. Once you find an article, print it off or cut it out. Fill out the information, and then write a one page summary of the article. Bring this sheet along with the printed article to class.

The topic of an article you are to look for is on **'Treaties with Tribal Land,' 'Dakota Access Pipeline,'** or **'Bears Ears.'**

Title of Article:
Written By:
Media Source:
Date:
Tribe Affected:

Summary:_____

_____

_____

_____

_____

_____

_____

_____

_____

_____

_____

_____

_____

_____

_____

_____

_____

10.
Lesson 7: Mascots

Lesson: Mascots **Standards:** NCSS: Theme 2 NCSS: Theme 4 CCSS: Writing 1. Write arguments to support claims in an analysis of substantive topics or texts, using valid reasoning and relevant and sufficient evidence. CCSS: Listening and Speaking 1. Prepare for and participate effectively in a range of conversations and collaborations with diverse partners, building on others' ideas and expressing their own clearly and persuasively.	

Materials: Worksheets, timer
Time: 30-60 minutes, depending on grade level and depending on if you plan on having the students do the debate activity

Desired Outcomes

Learning Goals:
- I can explain the meaning of stereotypes and understand why some Natives feel Indian mascots perpetuate stereotypes.

Understandings: Students will be able to understand why some Natives feel using Natives as mascots perpetuates stereotypes, but also be given the chance to gain their own opinion on the topic.	**Essential Questions:** What are mascots? Why would Natives used as mascots be bad? How are Native mascots represented in sports? Do you think Native mascots accurately represent Native culture, or do they misrepresent the culture?
Students will know… (Knowledge & Vocab) Stereotypes are a preconceived notion, especially about a group of people.	**Students will be able to… (Skills)** • Utilize debate and reasoning skills • Utilize reading comprehension skills • Utilize listening, recall, and application skills • Utilize writing skills • Utilize research skills • Apply information learned to another tribe/situation

Evidence of Learning

Performance Tasks • Research their topic • Present topic stating their stance on topic • Essay on if their views have changed after studying and listening to both sides **Unit Project Assignment:** Research if there are any schools with Native mascots or symbols in the area. Find an article that is for and against using the mascot. If the student cannot find a local article or enough information, have them use a professional or college team in the area.	**Success Criteria** • I am able to list three pros and cons of each side of the debate. • I am able to generate my own conclusion from the debate and write a one page essay on why. • My essay is at least one page, 5 paragraphs. An introduction and conclusion paragraph with 3 supporting paragraphs.

Learning Plan

Lesson:

This is a very sensitive topic, and there are a lot of feelings and differences when talking about Native American mascots. Everyone has their own views, and even within Native culture the topic can be sensitive. With both older and younger grades, this is also a good chance to talk about stereotypes, and making assumptions about others.

A week or so before this lesson, give the class the hand out (located at the end of this lesson) that describes the debate you will be having in class. Draw names or assign half the class to be "For Native Mascots" and the other half to be "Against Native Mascots." If you have a Native student in your class, please be sensitive to their feelings and let them pick what side they would like to be on. If there is time at the end of class, a few days leading up to this debate, let the two groups meet together and talk about what things they have found, and decide who will talk and how to best argue their side.

On the day of this class, give each side 10 minutes to argue their side (20 minutes total).

When the debate is done, tell them how this topic may not seem like a very important topic, but for many Natives it is. For hundreds of years they have been trying to be acknowledged as people, and humans, and not as a fictional characters. Of all of the hundreds of mascots that are in schools and sports teams, Natives by far outnumber any other group of people being portrayed as mascots. Many of these mascot images portray very unflattering and demeaning pictures of Natives. They all have big noses, big teeth, and are red skinned. Usually they are depicted wearing ceremonial clothing and headdresses. Ask the following: Do you remember how we have been talking about the Native culture as a religion? How would you feel if something sacred to you was being depicted in a negative way? What if schools decided that their new mascot was going to be "Black Burglars," "Blackskins," "Rednecks," "Fighting Jews," "Brown Banditos," or "White Crackers?" Do you think any of these would pass the school board's approval? Why is it okay for Natives to be mascots?

"Now, in the twenty-first century, should any team, at any level or in any sport, continue to call itself the Indians? Or some stereotypical variation, like Braves or Redskins? Daniel Snyder, owner of the NFL's Washington Redskins, vows never to change his team's name. 'It represents honor,' he insists, 'represents respect, represents pride.'

Ray Halbritter, of the Oneida Indian Nation, sees it differently. 'Redskins is defined in the dictionary as an offensive label for Native Americans—that was used against them when they were forcibly removed from their lands at gunpoint,' Halbritter says. 'It's hard to believe that Washington's NFL team continues to use this name, even though it's the sort of slur that would never be used in polite conversation'" (Sheinkin 230).

For other teams, many of their symbols and actions used, like the tomahawk chop, are made up. So, how are we honoring something when it really isn't them at all? With Native mascots becoming so common place, many people overlook that these are real people, and not just characters. These characters are not who Natives are today. By romanticizing them, it perpetuates the stereotypes of who people think Natives are.

It is important for us to be educated on any culture before we make assumptions. This is what we should do for anyone in general. Should we decide to make fun of or mock someone before we get to know them?

Adaptations for younger grades:

Time: 20 minutes

Define the word **Stereotype**: a preconceived notion, especially about a group of people. Stereotypes are things that people think about you before they even know you, and they judge you based on who they think you are. For example, "All boys have stinky feet." Or "Girls all talk too much." Most of the time stereotypes are negative and not true. How do you feel when someone says something bad about you before they even know you? Do you think we need to be nice to everyone, and give people a chance to get to know you before we judge them?

Many Native Americans do not like Native Americans as mascots because the pictures they use are not very nice to Natives. When we use Natives as mascots and characters, people lose sight of the fact that Natives still exist today. Many of the actions, like the tomahawk chop, and images that they portray are not accurate.

This is also a good time to talk about bullying, and why we should be nice to everyone.

In the book *Mascots that Honor Indians: the Audacity of a Dope for Suggesting Schools Change their Indian Mascots*, it states:
"Research, both official and unofficial, has concluded that:
1. Most non-Indians know very little about Indian people.
2. Most schools teach very little about Indian people.
3. Schools with Indian mascots perpetuate racism and ignorance about Indian people.
4. Schools using Indian mascots can start by changing their mascots.
5. Schools have been encouraged to teach more about Indian people.
We join in encouraging schools to 'walk a mile' with us, and start by teaching students more about Indian tribes and peoples so that there can be greater understanding of what we are trying to accomplish. Hopefully, parents, teachers, and students will be better understanding our desire to end the racism and ignorance that is being perpetuated by Indian mascots (E. Zendejas, Edouardo 37).

Assignments: Have students write an essay describing an instance when someone judged them before getting to know them, and how it made them feel.

Or, hand out the debate sheet.

Essay: After listening to both sides of the debate, write an essay on which side "Indian mascots should not be used in schools" or "Indian mascots should be allowed to stay in schools" you most agree with and why? Make sure to cite evidence for your arguments.

Name: _____ Date: _____

The Great Debate!

For this debate you will be given a side of 'For' or 'Against.' Over the next week you will research online, in books, and in the media on whether or not schools should keep or get rid of the use of Native mascots. Come up with reasons to back your case to try and convince the other side that your side is the correct side.

Over the next week, you will be given time at the end of class to meet with the students on your side of the debate to share what you have discovered, and how to best present your information.

Date of the Debate: _____

The side of the debate I was given is:

_____ Indian mascots should be removed from schools.

_____ Schools should be allowed to keep their Indian mascots.

Notes:

11.

Lesson 8: Influential Native Americans Today

Lesson: Influential Native Americans Today
Standards:
NCSS: Theme 1
NCSS: Theme 3
CCSS: Writing
2. Write informative/explanatory texts to examine and convey complex ideas and information clearly and accurately through the effective selection, organization, and analysis of content.
7. Conduct short as well as more sustained research projects based on focused questions, demonstrating understanding of the subject under investigation.
8. Gather relevant information from multiple print and digital sources, assess the credibility and accuracy of each source, and integrate the information while avoiding plagiarism.
CCSS: Listening and Speaking
1. Prepare for and participate effectively in a range of conversations and collaborations with diverse partners, building on others' ideas and expressing their own clearly and persuasively

Materials: Printed worksheets, computer/internet, crayons, pencil/pen. Video *Medicine Women* (Available on PBS at www.pbs.org/video/medicine-woman-full-episode).
Suggested Books: Sheinkin, Steve. *Undefeated: Jim Thorpe and the Carlisle Indian School Football Team.* Summary: This book is about the life of Jim Thorpe and his rise to be one of the greatest athletes of all time. However, the book gives a greater understanding of when Jim was at boarding school, and it also talks about why the boarding school was started. This book is 233 pages, but an easy read for young readers.
Time: 30-60 minutes, depending on grade level, and time limited for computers

Desired Outcomes

Learning Goals:
- I can explain how Native Americans are contributing to our society today.

Understandings:	**Essential Questions:**
Students will understand that Native Americans exist today. They live like everyone else, and are making an impact on Native communities all across the US.	Do Native Americans still exist today? What role do they have in America today? Do you know any famous Native Americans?

Students will know... (Knowledge and Vocab)	**Students will be able to... (Skills)**
Students will get to know at least one of the influential Natives listed and be able to tell what they do and what they have done to help Native people.	• Utilize presentation skills • Utilize reading comprehension skills • Utilize listening, recall, and application skills • Utilize writing skills • Utilize research skills • Apply information learned to another tribe/situation

Evidence of Learning

Performance Tasks:	**Success Criteria**
• Native profile • Reading comprehension: Billy Mills • Research news article related to profile **Unit Project Assessment:** Find an individual from that tribe that has made a difference or helped the Native community today. Or research the most recent tribal Chairman. (This person must be living.)	• After researching my individual, I am able to state the following about a modern Native: Their tribe, what they are known for, obstacles they had to overcome to obtain their goals, awards they have been given for their work, and one interesting fact about this person.

Learning Plan

Lesson:

This is a fun lesson that can be presented in a few different ways. For younger kids, you can discuss biographies of different Natives and their accomplishments each day. You may want to look up their pictures to show the students.

For older kids, you can use a computer lab for the first half of the lesson. Assign each student a name to look up, or a pair/group of students if there are not enough names to go around. Have them fill out the worksheet as they find them on the computer. The last half of the class have students/groups present their findings.

Or, you can use this as homework and then have students present for the lesson. However, make sure that all of the names have been assigned so the students get to know about all of the different Natives.

Natives are still around today. They are educated, and striving to keep their culture while making a difference in their community. There are so many Natives doing so many wonderful things, it is hard to list them all. This is just a short list of Natives who have made a difference.

Use these short bios as a starting block for your lesson. It will help give you some background on each of the people as your students are researching (Sources cited in Reference section).

1. **Susan LaFlesche Picotte**, 1865–1915, Omaha Tribe of Nebraska. Susan is known as the first Native American to earn a medical degree. She set up a hospital on the Omaha reservation promoting good hygiene and health, and discouraging drinking.
2. **Billy Mills**, 1938– , Oglala Sioux. Billy is known as the only American to have ever won an Olympic gold medal in the 10,000 meters in track and field. He accomplished this achievement at the 1964 Tokyo games. He was an alternate on the team, running in borrowed shoes. Billy currently runs a foundation, Running Strong for American Indian Youth, that helps Native communities across the nation.
3. **Maria Tallchief**, 1925–2013, Osage. Maria was America's first major prima ballerina. She moved from her home in Oklahoma to California, and finally to New York City to try and advance her career. She met choreographer George Balanchine, who co-founded the New York City Ballet, and Maria became its first premier dancer. She played the lead in ballets such as *The Firebird* and *The Nutcracker*.
4. **Shoni Schimmel**, 1992– , Umatilla Nation. Shoni is a 5'9" shooting guard who was an All-American college basketball player for the University of Louisville. Shoni was also a first round draft pick for Atlanta Dream of the WNBA (Women's National Basketball Association).
5. **John Bennett Herrington**, 1958– , Chickasaw Nation. John is known for his accomplishment of being the first Native American to fly in space!
6. **Larry Echo Hawk**, 1948– , Pawnee Nation. Larry is an attorney and politician. In 2009, Larry joined President Barack Obama's administration as the United States Assistant Secretary of the Interior for Indian Affairs. Before that, he was elected Attorney General of Idaho. In 2012, he was called as a general authority for the Church of Jesus Christ of Latter-day Saints (LDS church).
7. **Louie Gong**, 1974– , Nooksack. Louie is a Native artist, public speaker, educator, and entrepreneur. He is most known for his shoe designs for Vans Shoes. Louie runs Eighth Generation, a company that promotes local Native art.
8. **Jeremy Thompson (Thompson Brothers)**, 1987– , Iroquois. Jeremy is known for his achievement as a professional lacrosse player, and is sponsored by Nike and N7 (N7 is Nike's shoe line for Natives). He is also featured in the documentary *Medicine Games* with his brother Hiana. All four brothers play lacrosse at a professional level and are known for being some of the best lacrosse players in the nation.
   1. **Miles Thompson**, 1990– , Iroquois. University of Albany, pro team Georgia Swarm
   2. **Lyle Thompson**, 1992– , Iroquois. University of Albany, pro team Georgia Swarm

3. **Hiana Thompson**, 1988– , Iroquois. Pro team Georgia Swarm

9. **Lori Arviso Alvord**, 1958– , Navajo (Diné). Lori is best known as being the first Navajo women to be a board certified surgeon.

10. **Adam Beach**, 1972– , Saulteaux. Adam is a Native actor best known for his role as Victor in *Smoke Signals*. Other films Adam has been in are *Windtalkers, Flags of Our Fathers,* and *Joe Dirt*. Adam also had a role as a detective in a few seasons of *Law and Order SVU*.

11. **Bronson Koenig**, 1994– , Ho-Chunk Nation. Bronson is basketball player that played for the Wisconsin Badgers. He then moved onto the NBA G league, playing for Grand Rapids Drive. He currently holds basketball clinics for Native youth.

12. **Ashton Locklear**, 1998– , Lumbee Tribe. Ashton is a gymnast who was an alternate for the U.S. women's Olympic gymnastics team in 2016. Ashton is an uneven bars specialist.

13. **Jim Thorpe**, 1887–1953, Sac and Fox. Jim was an Olympic athlete, winning gold in 1912 in the pentathlon and decathlon. He was the first Native to win gold for his country. Jim also played both football and baseball at the professional level.

14. **Cory Witherill**, 1971– , Navajo (Diné) is a race car driver for the Indy Racing League, Infiniti Pro Series, Indy Lights, and ARCA series.

15. **Notah Begay**, 1972– , Navajo (Diné). Notah is a professional golfer on the PGA tour. Currently, he is also an analyst for the Golf Channel.

16. **Wes Studi**, 1947– , Cherokee. Wes is an actor and film producer, best known for his role in *Last of the Mohicans*, and most recently *Hostiles*.

17. **Sam Bradford**, 1987– , Cherokee. Sam played football for the University of Oklahoma. As a sophomore, he became only the second sophomore to win the Heisman Trophy. Following his college career, Sam was the first overall pick in the 2010 NFL Draft. Sam has played for the St. Louis Rams, Philadelphia Eagles, and the Minnesota Vikings.

18. **Robbie Robertson**, 1943– , Cayuga and Mohawk. Robbie is known across Indian country as a rock and roll musician. He was inducted into the Rock and Roll Hall of Fame in 1994.

19. **Suzan Harjo**, 1945– , Cheyenne and Hodulgee Muscogee. Suzan is an advocate for Native American rights. She was a Congressional liaison for Indian affairs during the Jimmy Carter administration. Later she became the president of the National Council of American Indians. She is also known for helping with policy changes to get sports teams to drop Native mascots.

20. **Ben Nighthorse Campbell**, 1933– , Northern Cheyenne. Ben is a politician from Colorado. He served three terms as a United States Senator.

21. **Paulette Jordan**, 1979– , Coeur d'Alene. Paulette won the Democratic nomination in Idaho's governor's race in 2018.

22. **Sharice Davids**, 1980 - , HoChunk. Sharice is an attorney and politician who is serving in the U.S. House of Representatives for the Kansas 3rd Congressional District since 2019.

23. **Deb Haaland**, 1960 - Pueblo of Laguna. Deb is an attorney and politician who is serving in the U.S. House of Representatives for New Mexico 1st Congressional District since 2019.

- *Medicine Woman* is a good documentary to watch. You can find it on pbs.org. It is approximately 57 mins. Direct link to video: **www.pbs.org/video/medicine-woman-full-episode.**

Assignments:

1. Answers to the reading comprehension essay on Billy Mills:

    1-A, 2-10,000 meter race and marathon, 3-Varies, 4-C, 5-Varies

2. Native Profile: Assign students, alone or in groups, to research their assigned person. Draw or print a picture of that person, and fill out the rest of the questions on the sheet. This can be done in class at the computer lab, or at home. Students can also present in class what they have learned.

3. Presentation: Take the Native Profile one step further and have students create a poster and write-up.

Name: _____ Date: _____
Native Profile

Name:

Tribe(s):

```
Picture of me...                    What I am
                                    known for...
```

What obstacles did I have to overcome to achieve my goals?

Interesting fact about me...

Name: _____ Date: _____

Native Profile

Native profile research and presentation: You will either be assigned a name or pick one of the Natives off the following list. Use the internet or library to find information for that person, focusing on the questions listed. This will be presented in class.

_____ Susan LaFlesche Picotte, Doctor

_____ Billy Mills, Olympian

_____ Maria Tallchief, Ballerina

_____ Shoni Schimmel, Basketball

_____ John Bennett Herrington, Astronaut

_____ Larry Echo Hawk, Attorney/Politician

_____ Louie Gong, Artist

_____ Jeremy Thompson, Lacrosse

_____ Miles Thompson, Lacrosse

_____ Lyle Thompson, Lacrosse

_____ Hiana Thompson, Lacrosse

_____ Lori Arviso Alvord, Surgeon

_____ Paulette Jordan, Politician

_____ Adam Beach, Actor

_____ Bronson Koenig, Basketball

_____ Ashton Locklear, Gymnast

_____ Jim Thorpe, Olympian

_____ Cory Witherill, Race Car Driver

_____ Notah Begay, Golfer

_____ Wes Studi, Actor & Producer

_____ Sam Bradford, Football

_____ Robbie Robertson, Musician

_____ Suzan Harjo, Activist

_____ Ben Nighthorse Campbell, Politician

_____ Sharice Davids, Politician

_____ Deb Haaland, Politician

Make sure to include the following in your research:

1. Name
2. Tribe
3. Where is the tribe/reservation located?
4. What is this person known for? Or how have they helped their Native community?
5. What obstacles did they have to overcome to attain their goals?
6. Have they been given any awards for the work they have done?
7. What is one interesting fact about this person?

Due Date: _____

Name: _____ Date: _____

Natives in the News

Native Americans still exist today. Your assignment will be to make an effort to look for different Native American issues or people in the news. Use any media outlet that you have available. Once you find an article, print it off or cut it out. Fill out the information, and then write a one-page summary of the article. Bring this sheet along with the printed article to class.

The topic of an article you are to look for is on **'Native Profile.'** Search for any news articles that relate to the person you are assigned to profile.

Title of Article:
Written By:
Media Source:
Date:
Tribe Affected:

Summary:_____

_____

_____

_____

_____

_____

_____

_____

_____

_____

_____

_____

_____

_____

_____

_____

_____

Reading Comprehension - Billy Mills: The Path to the Medal

This essay is courtesy of Running Strong for American Indian Youth.

Billy Mills was born in Pine Ridge, South Dakota, and was raised on the impoverished Pine Ridge Indian Reservation for Oglala Sioux people. He was orphaned when he was twelve years old. Mills took up running while attending the Haskell Institute, which is now known as Haskell Indian Nations University in Lawrence, Kansas. Both a boxer and a runner in his youth, Mills gave up boxing to focus on running.

He attended the University of Kansas on an athletic scholarship, and was named an NCAA All-America cross-country runner three times. In 1960 he won the individual title in the Big Eight cross-country championships. The University of Kansas track team won the 1959 and 1960 outdoor national championships while Mills was on the team. While at the University of Kansas, he met and married his sweetheart, Patricia.

After graduating with a degree in Physical Education, Mills entered the United States Marine Corps. He was a First Lieutenant in the Marine Corps Reserve when he competed in the 1964 Tokyo Olympics.

Billy Mills qualified for the 1964 Summer Olympics on the U.S. Track and Field team in the 10,000 meter and the marathon. Mills was a virtual unknown. His winning time of 28:24.4 was almost 50 seconds faster than he had run before and set a new Olympic record for the event. No American had ever won the 10,000 meter before, nor has any American come close until Galen Rupp took silver at the 2012 London Olympics.

Despite going up against athletes such as Australian Ron Clarke, the reigning world record holder, Mills' belief in himself never wavered. His goal was to win. When the gun fired on race day, Mills hung with the leaders, despite a pace for the 10,000 meter race that was nearly as fast as his best for 5,000 meters. On the final lap, he found himself one of just three men in contention for the win, the other two being Clarke and Mohammed Gammoudi of Tunisia.

The bell lap played out like an obstacle course as the leaders weaved around nearly a dozen lapped runners. Billy was pushed off balance twice in the jostling for position. Stumbling into lane 2 in the aggressive fray, Billy seemed to fade out of contention on the backstretch when Gammoudi surged. Mills soon approached Patricia's seat about eight yards behind the leaders.

Coming off the curve of the straightaway, just under his wife's position, a lapped runner began to float wide, and Mills saw daylight: space to sprint for victory. He pumped his arms, lifted his knees, and gave it all he had. Glancing left at a lapped runner, Mills thought he saw an eagle on the competitor's singlet (jersey). He remembered words his father once told him, "The pursuit of a dream will heal your broken wings." He flew with the wings of an eagle to the finish line, breaking the tape first.

Since his gold medal race, Mills has become a co-founder of the nonprofit group, Running Strong for American Indian Youth, with Eugene Krizek. The aim of Running Strong is to help American Indian people fulfill their basic needs (food, water, and shelter), while also helping their communities gain self-sufficiency and self-esteem. He now acts as a spokesperson for the group and travels the country speaking out for and on behalf of Native American communities. Mills' charity work also includes diabetes prevention and management education for adults and especially for youth. Being a diabetes patient himself, Mills helps people with diabetes learn how to maintain a healthy lifestyle and improve their lives.

Billy Mills

Name:_____ Date: _____

1. Growing up, Billy Mills had a lot of things he had to overcome. Which was not something he experienced?
      a. His dog died when he was 12.
      b. He was raised in a community that was very poor.
      c. Both of his parents died when he was young.

2. What events did Mills compete in at the Olympics? Use text evidence to support your answer.

3. During the race, Mills said he "saw daylight." What did he mean by that? Use text evidence to support your answer.

4. During the race, Mills remembers what his father once told him, "The pursuit of a dream will heal your broken wings." What do you think he meant by those words?
      a. All your dreams will come true.
      b. You should always try to win the race.
      c. When you achieve your goals, it will make you a better and happier person.

5. How does Mills use his experiences to now help other Native communities have a better life? Use text evidence to support your answer.

12.
Lesson 9: Code Talkers

Lesson: Code Talkers **Standards:** NCSS: Theme 5 CCSS: Writing 7. Conduct short as well as more sustained research projects based on focused questions, demonstrating understanding of the subject under investigation. 8. Gather relevant information from multiple print and digital sources, assess the credibility and accuracy of each source, and integrate the information while avoiding plagiarism. 9. Draw evidence from literary or informational texts to support analysis, reflection, and research. CCSS Reading 3. Analyze how and why individuals, events, and ideas develop and interact over the course of a text.
Materials: Worksheets, essay on John Brown, Jr., and optional books *The Unbreakable Code* and *The Navajo Code Talkers*. **Suggested Books:** Hoagland Hunter, Sara. *The Unbreakable Code.* Summary: Because John is afraid to leave the Navajo Reservation, his grandfather explains to him how the Navajo language, faith, and ingenuity helped win World War II. **Time:** 30-60 minutes, depending on grade

Desired Outcomes

Learning Goals:
- I can explain how Navajo Code Talkers impacted the outcome of WWII.

Understandings: Students will understand the facts leading up to WWII, and why the U.S. government felt it necessary to enter the war. They will also understand how Native tribes were able to create a successful code during WWI. The success of the first code helped the government decide to enlist the help of the Navajo to create a new code to help with WWII. The Navajo Code Talkers and their mission during the war were so highly classified, it was not declassified until 1968, 23 years after the war had ended.	**Essential Questions:** What was happening during WWII when the U.S. decided to enter? What was the U.S. government's solution to the Japanese breaking all of their codes? What was the Navajo Code Talkers' role during the war?
Students will know... (Knowledge & Vocab) The Navajo Code Talkers created an unbreakable code. This code was used during WWII. The Navajo used Navajo words to describe military terms. The Code Talkers were sent all over the world, even in the middle of the battle fields to help transmit messages.	**Students will be able to... (Skills)** - Utilize debate and reasoning skills - Utilize reading comprehension skills - Utilize listening, recall, and application skills - Utilize writing skills - Utilize research skills - Apply information learned to another tribe/situation

Evidence of Learning

Performance Tasks - Decoding worksheet - Reading comprehension essay and questions **Unit Project Assignment:** Research an individual from the past who has made a difference in the Native community.	**Success Criteria** - I am able to apply coding skills to successfully decode the message. - I am able to use text evidence to answer the six questions related to the essay correctly. - I am able to research and explain how someone from my chosen tribe made a difference in society.

Learning Plan

Lesson:

Recap of what was going on during WWII before the Natives got involved *(use your own summary or the one below)*:

World War II spanned the years 1939 to 1945. It is known as the deadliest and one of the most expensive wars fought in history. More than 50 countries took part in the war, and most of the world felt the effects of it (britannica.com).

After our experience with World War I, the United States hoped to stay out of the fight. Congress passed a series of Neutrality Acts between 1935 and 1939. In December 1941, Japan bombed Pearl Harbor in hopes of expansion in the Far East. Because of this attack, the United States could no longer stay out of the conflict. By 1942, all of the major countries were involved in the war (britannica.com).

After entering the war, the United States had a problem with getting ahead of Japanese attacks. The United States created different codes to try and communicate without the Japanese knowing what they were doing. However, every code they created was broken by the Japanese.

During WWI, the Choctaw and other tribes were recruited to transmit messages in their tribal language. After seeing the great success of those codes, the Marine Corps enlisted the help of the Navajo in 1941 and 1942. The Marine Corps enlisted 29 Navajo men to develop a code within the Navajo language. Once the code was developed and the war progressed, the Marine Corps enlisted more than 400 Navajos to become Code Talkers. A Code Talking school was established to help the 400 men learn the code, and help them in the battlefield (National Museum of the American Indian).

Being able to keep the messages secret made the difference between winning and losing the battle. The Code Talkers did more than just talk on radio equipment. Code Talkers needed to know how to set up and maintain the equipment. They were also given the messages in English and had to memorize and send in Navajo. The Code Talkers were sent all over the world, even in the middle of the battlefields to help transmit messages. Because of their efforts, and because of so many others, the war was finally over in September 1945 (National Museum of the American Indian).

On July 26, 2001, President George W. Bush invited 21 of the remaining Code Talkers to the White House to give them a medal of honor. In President Bush's speech, released from the White House Press, he stated:

"Today, America honors 21 Native Americans who, in desperate hour, gave their country a service only they could give. In war, using their native language, they relayed secret messages that turned the course of battle. At home, they carried for decades the secret of their own heroism. Today we give these exceptional Marines the recognition they earned so long ago.

America pays tribute to the tradition and community that produced such men, the great Navajo Nation. The paintings in this rotunda tell of America and its rise as a nation. Among them are the images of the first Europeans to reach the coast, and the first explorer to come upon the Mississippi.

But before all these firsts on this continent, there were the first people. They are depicted in the background, as if extras in the story. Yet, their own presence here in America predates all human record. Before others arrived, the story was theirs alone.

Today we mark a moment of shared history and shared victory. We recall a story that all Americans can celebrate, and every American should know. It is a story of ancient people, called to serve in a modern war. It is a story of one unbreakable oral code of the Second World War, messages traveling by field radio on Iwo Jima in the very language heard across the Colorado plateau centuries ago.

Above all, it's a story of young Navajos who brought honor to their nation and victory to their country. Some of the Code Talkers were very young, like Albert Smith, who joined the Marines at 15. In order to enlist, he said, I had to advance my age a little bit. At least one code talker was over-age, so he claimed to be younger in order to serve. On active duty, their value was so great, and their order so sensitive, they were closely guarded. By war's end, some 400 Navajos had served as Code Talkers. Thirteen were killed in action, and their names, too, are on today's roll of honor.

Regardless of circumstances, regardless of history, they came forward to serve America. The Navajo code itself provides a part of the reason. Late in his life, Albert Smith explained, the code word for America was, "Our Mother." Our Mother stood for freedom, our religion, our ways of life, and that's why we went in. The Code Talkers joined 44,000 Native Americans who wore the uniform in World War II. More than 12,000 Native Americans fought in WWI. Thousands more served in Korea, Vietnam and serve to this very day.

Gentlemen, your service inspires the respect and admiration of all Americans, and our gratitude is expressed for all time, in the medals it is now my honor to present" (The White House).

Discussion:
- Why were the Navajo needed in the War? What was the special skill they were able to offer?
- What was the Navajo code word for America? And why did they choose that word to represent America?
- How many men were the "Original Code Talkers," the ones who developed the code?
- How many Navajo men were enlisted to become Code Talkers?

Read and discuss the bio of the Code Talker, John Brown, Jr., as part of the lesson, or use as an assignment.

Learn some code:
Code Talkers used the Navajo Language to represent different military terms. For example, they used different kinds of birds to represent the different planes. They also used the names of different fish to represent different ships. The following is a list of a few codes they had to memorize:

Military Term	Navajo Word (pronunciation)	English Translation
Dive Bomber	Gini	Chicken Hawk
Torpedo Plane	Tas-chizzie	Swallow
Fighter Plane	Da-he-tih-hi	Hummingbird
Bomber Plane	Jay-sho	Buzzard
Patrol Plane	Ga-gih	Crow
Transport	Atsah	Eagle
Battleship	Lo-tso	Whale
Aircraft	Tsidi-moffa-ye-hi	Bird Carrier

Submarine	Besh-lo	Iron Fish
Minesweeper	Cha	Beaver
Destroyer	Ca-lo	Shark
Cruiser	Lo-tso-yazzie	Small Whale

(Central Intelligence Agency)

Adjustments for younger and older students:
- For older students, add more content to the history and background of what was going on during World War II. This lesson can be taught while teaching about WWII.
- For younger students, focus more on how the Navajo code was able to help America in a time when it was needed the most. Read *The Unbreakable Code* listed as a suggested book at the beginning of the lesson. Use the book as a way to teach the events of WWII and about Code Talkers. Use the info in lesson as needed. Teach a few of the codes to the students.
- Use the essays on the Code Talkers as a discussion topic, or for reading comprehension practice. ANSWERS: 1-19, 2-B, 3-1968, 4-A, 5&6-Varies
- CODE ANSWER: Navajo Code Talkers created an unbreakable code.

Name: _____ Date: _____

Crack the Code

The Navajo Code Talkers created a code that no one was able to break! They used Navajo words as code for military terms. The Japanese were not able to break the Code Talkers code, let's see if you can break this code. Use the letter and numbers below to find the hidden message.

A= 1	G= 7	M= 13	S= 19	Y= 25
B= 2	H= 8	N= 14	T= 20	Z= 26
C= 3	I= 9	O= 15	U= 21	
D= 4	J= 10	P= 16	V= 22	
E= 5	K= 11	Q= 17	W= 23	
F= 6	L= 12	R= 18	X= 24	

___ ___ ___ ___ ___ ___   ___ ___ ___ ___
14 1 22 1 10 15   3 15 4   5

___ ___ ___ ___ ___ ___ ___   ___ ___ ___ ___ ___ ___ ___
20 1 12 11 5 18 19   3 18 5 1 20 5 4

___ ___   ___ ___ ___ ___ ___ ___ ___ ___ ___ ___
 1 14   21 14 2 18 5 1 11 1 2 12 5

___ ___ ___ ___ .
 3 15 4 5

Rewrite the sentence you decoded:

_____

_____

John Brown, Jr.

Written by Crystal Tewa Begay. Crystal is the granddaughter of John Brown, Jr. She lives in Utah, with her husband and 5 children. Photos used with permission of Crystal Tewa Begay.

My name is Crystal Tewa Begay. I am of the Tangle Clan, born for the McCombs Scottish Clan and my maternal grandfather is of the Coyote Pass Clan. I was born and raised on the Navajo Reservation. I grew up learning about my beautiful heritage and learning to speak our unique language. I grew up knowing that my maternal grandpa was a hero! I was taught as a young child the many wonderful contributions he made not only to our Navajo Tribe, but also to our country.

My grandpa's name was John Brown, Jr. He was born in Canyon de Chelly, near Chinle, Arizona, on December 24, 1921. John attended Chinle Boarding School as a child and then went on to graduate high school from Albuquerque Indian School in 1940. He was about 19 when WWII began. He and his young Navajo friends were playing basketball when he heard about the bombing of Pearl Harbor. He was approached by recruiters from the United States Marines Corps who told him about a great war going on far away from his Navajo homeland. He wanted to help and made the decision to enlist in the United States Marine Corps.

After he arrived for training, his all-Navajo platoon was told they were there for a special mission: to devise a secret code in their Native language. In May 1942, the first 29 Navajo recruits attended boot camp, where they created the Navajo Code. The code was complicated and proved to be unbreakable. Using their Navajo language, they implemented words for animals to represent warcraft and weapons. They used Navajo words in place of different military terms in such a way that confused even the most skilled cryptographer.

During the course of the war, they were able to send and receive secret messages over the radios and telephones about enemy plans and other classified information in a code that the Japanese never broke. Navajo Code Talkers took part in every U.S. Marine Corps battle in the Pacific from 1942-1945. They were credited with playing a very important role in the Battle of Iwo Jima. Major Howard Connor, 5th Marine Division Signal Officer, said, "Were it not for the Navajos, the Marines would never have taken Iwo Jima."

During the course of the War, the Navajo Code Talkers were sworn to secrecy. They were forbidden to tell anyone about the work they had done—not even their families. Even after the war, they never spoke of their role. It was not until 1968 that this information was declassified. In 2001, 56 years after WWII, John and four of the remaining Original Navajo Code Talkers were awarded the Congressional Gold Medal of Honor, awarded to them by President George W. Bush. Code Talkers who were trained and came after the Original 29, were awarded the Congressional Silver Medal.

My grandpa was asked to speak at this great event, held in the historic Capitol Rotunda. In his speech on behalf of the Code Talkers, he said he was, "Proud that the Navajo language bestowed on them as a Holy People was used to save American lives and help defeat U.S. enemies. As Code Talkers and Marines, we did our part to protect freedom and Democracy for the American people." He went on to say, "It is my hope that our young people will carry on this honorable tradition as long as the grass shall grow and the rivers flow."

Upon returning home from the war, John trained as a welder, became a journeyman, master carpenter, and cabinetmaker. In 1962, he became a member of the Navajo Tribal Council, representing the Crystal, New Mexico, community until 1982. He also served three terms as Crystal House Chapter President. He retired from the Navajo Nation Social Services as a Traditional Counselor in 2001. John Brown, Jr. passed away on May 20, 2009 in his home in Crystal, New Mexico. He was a very influential person among his Navajo people and had many wonderful experiences traveling around to various places to share the experiences he had as a Navajo Code Talker.

John Brown Jr.

Name:_____ Date:_____

1. How old was John Brown, Jr. when WWII started? Use text evidence to support your answer.

2. John Brown, Jr.'s platoon was given a special mission. What was their mission?
      a. To recruit more Navajos to enlist in the war.   b. Develop a code using their Native language.
      c. To win the Battle of Iwo Jima.   d. Their mission was classified.

3. What year did the Code Talkers mission finally become declassified? Use text evidence to explain your answer.

4. Which U.S. President gave the Code Talkers the Congressional Medal of Honor?
      a. George W. Bush   b. Bill Clinton
      c. Richard Nixon   d. John F. Kennedy

5. Why do you think their mission was classified, and they were not allowed to say anything, not even to their families? Use text evidence to explain your answer.

6. What did John Brown, Jr. do after the war? Use text evidence to explain your answer.

13.
Lesson 10: Storytelling/Creation

Lesson: Storytelling/Creation **Standards:** NCSS Theme 1 CCSS: Reading 9. Analyze how two or more texts address similar themes or topics in order to build knowledge or to compare the approaches the authors take. CCSS: Writing 7.Conduct short as well as more sustained research projects based on focused questions, demonstrating understanding of the subject under investigation. 8. Gather relevant information from multiple print and digital sources, assess the credibility and accuracy of each source, and integrate the information while avoiding plagiarism. 9. Draw evidence from literary or informational texts to support analysis, reflection, and research.
Materials: Naming assignment. Books. **Suggested Books:** Palmer, Merry M. *The Creator and Coyote: A Ute Mountain Ute Tale.* Jackson, Jake. *Native American Myths.* MacFarlan, Allan A. *Native American Tales and Legends.* Alexie, Sherman. *Thunder Boy Jr.* Summary: Thunder Boy Jr wants a name that will celebrate something cool that he has done. His dad honors him with a new name, a name that is sure to light up the sky. Echo Hawk, Terry. *Call Me Little Echo Hawk.* Summary: A grandfather teachers his granddaughter about how their family received the name "Echo Hawk" and why they should always be proud of who they are and where the come from. **Time:** 30-60 minutes, depending on grade

Desired Outcomes

Learning Goals:
- I can explain the different creation stories of how the different tribes believed they came to the earth.
- I can explain the importance of a name for a Native American.

Understandings: Students will understand what oral tradition is, and some of the stories from a few tribes on how they believe their people came to this earth. Students will also know about the importance of a name. There are stories and traditions behind names within the Native American culture.	**Essential Questions:** What are origin stories? Are the origin stories the same for all tribes? Why are names important? Who gives us our names?
Students will know... (Knowledge and Vocab) Oral tradition is the practice of passing down beliefs, traditions, or stories through spoken word, rather than writing them down. Origin stories, or creation stories, are about how each tribe believes their people were placed on the earth. Naming stories are stories of how people got their names.	**Students will be able to... (Skills)** - Utilize compare and contrast skills - Utilize listening, recall, and application skills - Utilize writing skills - Utilize research skills - Apply information learned to another tribe/situation

Evidence of Learning

Performance Tasks - Name worksheet - Compare and contrast worksheet	**Success Criteria** - I am able to explain my chosen tribe's creation story. - I am able to compare and contrast creation

Unit Project Assignment: Research and find your tribe's creation/origin story.	stories of different tribes. • I can explain the significance of a Native American name. • I researched the significance of my own name.

Learning Plan

Origin Stories (Creation):

Oral Tradition: Oral tradition is the practice of passing down beliefs, traditions, or stories through spoken word rather than writing them down. Native Americans have passed down stories and traditions as far back as anyone can remember. Stories have been told from generation to generation with the hope that they will always be remembered. Native Americans have stories about everything. They have stories about why the rabbit has long ears; they have stories about coyote, and about the bear. Natives have stories about dances, how to perform certain ceremonies, about people, and they have stories about how people were brought to this earth.

Stories are very important for Native Americans. Even today parents will tell their children of the stories they were told from their parents as a child. Telling stories is a way to help Natives keep their culture and their heritage going and remembered for many years to come. Native stories are not myths, they are not make believe, but are a real part of their history. Stories may change from storyteller to storyteller, or from one tribe to another. But the purpose or outcome of the story never changes.

Origin Stories, or creation stories, are stories about how each tribe believes their people were placed on the earth. There are over 500 different tribes in the United States, and each of those 500 plus tribes have their own creation story. Not one is the same. Some stories may be similar, but some are very different.

The following stories are from three different tribes, but you can get creation stories from any tribe. Most tribes have websites with tribal stories, and many have their creation story as one listed.

Omaha Origin Story

This version of the legend comes from Fletcher and LaFlesche, 1911 collection, The Omaha Tribe.

In the beginning, the people were in water. They opened their eyes but they could see nothing. As the people came out of the water, they beheld the day. As they came forth from the water, they were naked and without shame. But after many days passed, they desired covering. They took the fiber of weeds and grass and wove it about their loins for covering.

The people dwelt near a large body of water, in a wooded country where there was game. The men hunted the deer with clubs; they did not know the use of the bow. And the people thought, "What shall we do to help ourselves?" They began chipping stones; they found a bluish stone that was easily flaked and chipped and they made knives and arrowheads out of it. They now had knives and arrows, but they suffered from the cold and the people thought, "What shall we do?" A man found an elm root that was very dry and dug a hole in it and put a stick in and rubbed it. Then smoke came. He smelled it. Then the people smelled it and came near; others helped him to rub. At last a spark came; they blew this into flame and so fire came to warm the people and to cook their food. After this the people built grass houses, they cut the grass with the shoulder blade of a deer. Now the people had fire and ate their meat roasted; but they tired of roast meat and the people thought, "How should we have our meat cooked differently?" A man found a bunch of clay that stuck well together, then he brought sand to mix with it, then he molded it as a vessel. Then he gathered grass and set it on fire, and made the clay vessel hard. Then, after a time, he put water into the vessel and it held water. This was good. So he put water into the vessel and then meat into it and put the vessel over the fire and the people had boiled meat to eat.

Their grass coverings would fuzz and drop off. It was difficult to gather and keep these coverings. The people were dissatisfied and again the people thought, "What can we do to have something different to wear?" Heretofore they had been throwing away the hides they had taken from the game. So they took their stone knives to scrape down the hides and made them thin; they rubbed the hides with grass and with their hands to make them soft and then used the hides for clothing. Now they had clothing and were comfortable.

The women had to break the dry wood to keep up the fires; the men had some consideration for the women and sought plans for their relief. So they made the stone ax with a groove, and put a handle on the ax and fastened it with rawhide. This was used. But they wanted something better for breaking wood. So they made wedges of stone.

The grass shelter became unsatisfactory and the people thought, "How shall we better ourselves?" So they substituted bark for grass as a covering for their dwellings.

The people were determined to put skins on the poles of their dwellings. They tried the deerskin, but they were too small. They tried the elk, but both deer and elk skins became hard and unmanageable under the influence of the sun and rain. So they abandoned the use of the skins and returned to bark as a covering for their houses.

Until they had the buffalo, the people could not have good tents. They took one of the leg bones of the deer, splintered it, and made it sharp for an awl and with sinew sewed the buffalo skin and made comfortable tent covers.

Then a man, in wandering about, found some kernels, blue, red, and white. He thought he had secured something of great value, so he concealed them in a mound. One day he thought he would go to see if they were safe. When he came to the mound he found it covered with stalks having ears bearing kernels of these colors. He took an ear of each kind and gave the rest to the people to experiment with. They tried it for food, and found it good, and have ever since called it their life. As soon as the people found the corn good, they thought to make mounds like that in, which the kernels had been found. So they took the shoulder blade of the elk and built mounds like the first and buried the corn in them. So the corn grew and the people had abundant food.

In their wanderings, the people reached the forests where the birch trees grow and where there were great lakes. Here they made birch-bark canoes and traveled in them about the shores of the lakes. A man in his wanderings discovered two young animals and carried them home. He fed them and they grew large and were docile. He discovered that these animals would carry burdens, so a harness was fixed on them to which poles were fastened and they became the burden bearers. Before this every burden had to be carried on the back. The people bred the dogs and they were a help to the people.

Osage Creation Story
This version of the legend comes from Native American Myths *by Jake Jackson.*
Way beyond, once upon a time, some of the Osage lived in the sky. They did not know where they came from, so they went to Sun. They said, "From where did we come?"

He said, "You are my children."
Then they wandered still further and came to Moon.
Moon said, "I am your mother; Sun is your father. You must go away from here. You must go down to earth and live there."
So they came to the earth but found it covered with water. They could not return up above. They wept, but no answer came to them. They floated about in the air, seeking help from some god; but they found none.

Now all the animals were with them. Elk was the finest and most stately. They all trusted Elk. So they called to Elk, "Help us."

Then Elk dropped into the water and began to sink. Then he called to the winds. The winds came from all sides and they blew until the waters went upwards, as in a mist. Now before that the winds had traveled in only two directions; they went from north to south and from south to north. But when Elk called to them, they came from the east, from the north, from the west, and from the south. They met at a central place; then they carried the waters upwards.

Now at first the people could only see the rocks. So they traveled on the rocky places. But nothing grew there and there was nothing to eat. Then the waters continued to vanish. At last the people could see the soft earth. When Elk saw the earth, he was so joyous, he rolled over and over on the earth. Then all the loose hairs clung to the soil. So the hairs grew, and from them sprang beans, corn, potatoes, and wild turnips, and at last all the grasses and trees.

Now the people wandered over the land. They found human footsteps. They followed them. They joined with them, and traveled with them in search for food.

The Hoga came down from above, and found the earth covered with water. They flew in every direction. They sought for gods who would help them and drive the water away. They found not one. Then Elk came. He had a loud voice and he shouted to the four corners of the sky. The four winds came in answer. They blew upon the water and it vanished upwards, in a mist. Then the people could see the rocks. Now there was only little space on the rocks. They knew they must have more rom. The people were crowded. So they sent Muskrat down into the water. He did not come back. He was drowned. Then they sent Loon down. He did not come back. He was drowned. Then they sent Beaver down into the water. The water was too deep. Beaver was drowned. Then Crawfish dived into the water. He was gone a long time. When he came up there was a little mud in his claws. Crawfish was so tired he died. But the people took the mud out of his claws and made the land.

Ute Creation Story: The Creator and Coyote
This version of the legend comes from The Creator and Coyote: A Ute Mountain Ute Tale, a*dapted by Merry M. Palmer.*

In the days even before the ancient times, only the Creator and Coyote lived on the earth. They had come out of the light so long ago that no one remembered when or how.

The Creator wanted to form more people on the earth, so he gave Coyote a bag of sticks and said, "Carry these over the far hills to the valleys beyond. This is a great responsibility. You must not open the bag for any reason until you reach the sacred grounds."

"What am I carrying?" Coyote asked.

"I will say no more," the Creator answered. "Now be about your task."

Coyote was young and foolish and very, very curious. As soon as he walked over the first hill, out of sight from the Creator, he stopped. "It won't hurt to peek inside the bag," he thought.

As he loosened the string, people rushed for the opening of the bag and burst out. They yelled in strange languages of every kind.

Coyote tried to catch the people, but they ran away in many different directions. By the time he got the string tied again, he had lost many of the people. Worried about what he had done, Coyote tramped to the sacred valley and dumped out the few remaining people. Coyote returned to the Creator. "I have finished my task," he said, but he could not look the Creator in the eyes. "I know," the Creator said, searching his face. "You do not understand the terrible thing you have done."

"I tried to catch them," Coyote whined, hanging his head, "but they scared me. They spoke in strange tongues which I could not understand." "Those you let escape will forever war with the Utes," the Creator said, looking toward the distant hills. "They will be a thorn in the side of the chosen ones. The Utes, however, will always remain the mightiest and most valiant of heart." The Creator turned back to the Coyote. "You are irresponsible," he said, shaking his finger at him. "From this time on, you are doomed to wander the earth on all fours as a night prowler."

Discussion:
- What was the common theme in those stories?
- What was different about those stories?

Naming Stories

For a Native American, their name is very special. Their name tells a lot about the person. A long time ago, those names were given out of honor and pride. And it is still true today. Today when a child is born his parents will give him a name. Most of the time the name is given to the child because the parents like the sound of the name. However, as the child gets older, it is tradition to give the child a second name. This name is a name that they always remember and keep sacred in their heart, but they can still be called the name their parents gave them at birth. How the name is given is different for each tribe. Most of the time, a naming ceremony is done by blessing the child. With some tribes, this name is so sacred, they are not allowed to repeat their name, for other tribes, it is not and tribal members use their name when they introduce themselves.

Read the two stories about Native American names:
- *Thunder Boy Jr.* by Sherman Alexie
- *Call Me Little Echo Hawk* by Terry Echo Hawk

Please Note: These naming ceremonies are sacred ceremonies and are religious in nature. Please *do not* attempt to have a student assignment be, "Come up with your own Indian name."

Adaptations for younger grades:
- This lesson is good for both younger and older grades.
- If you have time, you may want to look up creation stories of the tribes in your area to read instead.

Assignments

After you have read the stories, explain their homework. They are to go home and ask their parents/guardians about their own name, and learn why their parents decided to name them that. Have them learn about the importance of their own name.

Name: _____ Date: _____

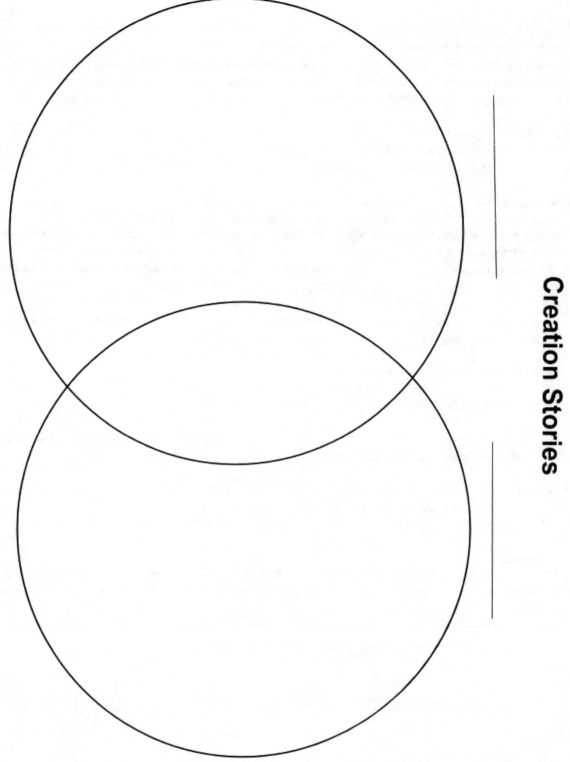

Creation Stories

Name: _____ Date: _____

My Name

Names are very special for Native Americans. The name they have tells a lot about the person they are. Your assignment is to interview your mom or dad, or whoever named you, and ask them about your name.

My full name:

My first name:

Why was I was given this name:

My middle name (or nickname):

Why was I was given this name:

My last name is:

The countries my ancestors came from:

Am I named after anyone special?

14.

Lesson 11: Dance & Regalia

Lesson: Dance and Regalia
Standards:
NCSS: Theme 1
CCSS: Listening & Speaking
2. Integrate and evaluate information presented in diverse media and formats, including visually, quantitatively, and orally.
CCSS: Writing
Gather relevant information from multiple print and digital sources, assess the credibility and accuracy of each source, and integrate the information while avoiding plagiarism.
CCSS Reading
7. Integrate and evaluate content presented in diverse media and formats, including visually and quantitatively, as well as in words.
Utah:
Standard 4.V.CO.1: Create works of art that reflect community cultural traditions.
Standard 4.M.R.4: Describe feelings or imagery conveyed by a music selection.

Materials: Copies of color page. Markers/crayons. Whiteboard and markers. Dance video.
(For a video of the different dances, go on Facebook and 'Like' the page "Dancing Strong Youth Pow Wow." In their videos tab, there is a video named "Teachers: This is the video that goes along with the lesson plan." It is a 6-minute video that shows the different dances talked about in the lesson. The video is not linked to YouTube, so you should be able to download it to your computer.) Another option is to search for different dance videos on the internet.
Suggested Book: Smith, Cynthia Leitich. *Jingle Dancer.* Summary: Jenna wants to be a jingle dancer, but she needs to find jingles for her regalia. As she finds her jingles, she comes to realize why and who she is dancing for. Duncan, Violet. *When We Dance.* Summary: A mother teaches her baby, Little Leaf, the reasons why they dance, and the importance of dance.
Time: 30-60 minutes, depending on grade

Desired Outcomes

Learning Goals:
* I can explain the differences between varying dances and Native regalia.

Understandings:	**Essential Questions:**
Students will know what a powwow is. They will know the different dances that are done at powwows. And they will know how to tell the difference between each dance.	What are powwows today? What is regalia? And what do the symbols mean on the dancers' clothes? What are the different dances? How can you tell what each dance is? What are traditions? What are traditions you have with your family?

Students will know... (Knowledge & Vocab)

Traditions – The handing down of statements, beliefs, legends, customs, information, etc., from generation to generation, especially by word of mouth or by practice.

Cultural Traditions – Beliefs or customs instituted and maintained by societies or governments.

Regalia – Traditional clothing worn by Native Americans.

Clan – A group of families within a tribe.

Tribe – In the United States, an Indian tribe, Native American tribe, tribal nation, or similar concept is an extant or historical clan, tribe, band, nation, or other group or community of indigenous peoples in the United States.

Students will be able to... (Skills)
* Utilize listening, recall, and application skills
* Utilize writing skills
* Utilize research skills
* Apply information learned to another tribe/situation

Intertribal – Involving members of more than one tribe. Often referred to at powwows when everyone comes together for a social dance.

Powwow – A Native American gathering involving feasting, singing, and dancing.

Shawl – A piece of fabric worn by women over the shoulders. A shawl is used when women dance the women's fancy shawl dance, or draped across their arm for the women's southern cloth traditional dance.

Bustle – A traditional part of the men's regalia worn during dance exhibitions. In modern form, the men's bustle is typically made of a string of eagle or hawk feathers attached to a backboard.

Roach – Is a traditional male headdress made up of porcupine, deer, or moose hair. They are most often worn by dancers at powwows.

Moccasins – A soft leather slipper or shoe, traditionally worn by Native Americans.

Grass – A men's style dance depicting the movement of the prairie grass. Originated with the Omaha Tribe of Nebraska.

Jingle – A women's healing dance that originated with the Ojibwe tribe.

Fancy – A term used for both a men's and women's style of dance. It is typically a fast and upbeat dance.

Hoop – A traditional dance that tells a story using hoops to make different shapes of birds, plants, and animals.

Evidence of Learning

Performance Tasks
- Design their own regalia.
- Students will write an essay stating why they chose the dance/regalia, and what each of the symbols mean.

Unit Project Assignment: Find a picture of a person at a powwow online (in any dance style they choose). Have students print and then label each part of the regalia. Or, have students research the traditional regalia worn by their specific tribe today.

Success Criteria
- I am able to explain why I chose the regalia and why I designed it.
- I am able to write at least one page on why I chose the dance, and what each symbol means on the regalia.

Learning Plan

Lesson:
What are traditions? The handing down of statements, beliefs, legends, customs, information, etc., from generation to generation, especially by word of mouth or by practice.

What are some traditions that you have in your family? What are cultural traditions? They are beliefs or customs instituted and maintained by societies or governments.

Native Americans have traditions. Their traditions have been passed down from generation to generation for a long time. They pass their traditions with stories, with their clothes, food, and with their dances. Native Americans don't live in teepees any more, and they don't hunt buffalo for their meals every night. They go to stores, and live in homes. However, like a lot of other cultures, they like to pass on their traditions to their children.

"Dances have always been a very important part of the life of the American Indian. Most dances seen at powwows today are social dances which might have had different meanings in earlier days. Although dance styles and content have changed, their meaning and importance has not. The outfits worn by dancers, like the styles of clothing today evolve over time, it is not a stagnant culture, but a vibrant and changing way of life" (powwows.com).

Today we are going to talk about the different dances and clothes that Natives wear.

What do you think a Native boy would wear to school? He would wear clothes like jeans, shirt, and tennis shoes. What do you think he would wear to a traditional dance? He would wear something called regalia. It is not a costume, or something he would wear every day. It is something he would wear on special occasions.

One of the places Native Americans wear their regalia is to a powwow. Have any of you heard of that word before? Powwow is used for a lot of different reasons. For Native Americans, a powwow is a gathering. It is where a lot of different Natives gather from different tribes. Powwows used to be just for when they were celebrating something, preparing for a hunt, or celebrating the harvest. Some powwows are still those things. Most Powwows today are dance competitions. They have judges and drum groups, and the dancers come together and compete to see who is the best dancer.

"In Indian Country, we define it as a cultural event that features group singing and dancing by men, women, and children. Through these gatherings, cultural traditions are passed from generation to generation. Skilled Native American artisans travel across the country to attend various Powwows to display and sell their handmade goods. It is a welcome opportunity to visit with friends and relatives, renew acquaintances, and trade or sell Native arts and crafts including jewelry, pottery, moccasins, ribbon shirts, shawls, dream catchers, and paintings. Above all, Powwows are a time to preserve traditions, to sing to the Creator, and to dance to the heartbeat of the drum" (The Nanticoke Indian Tribe).

At each powwow, the girls have three different dances they compete in, and the boys have three different dances they compete in. The regalia the dancers wear is different depending on what dance they do.

The Girls Dances: Jingle, Fancy Shawl, Traditional

The Boys Dances: Grass, Fancy, Traditional

The following are the stories and origin of the dances. **The stories and origins of the dances may vary by tribe and region.** The video mentioned at the beginning of the lesson will have a clip of each one. You can show the whole video at once, or each clip as you talk about each dance. The dances listed are in order of the video, along with the time stamp.

Women's Jingle: (*Time stamp from video - 0:06*)
The regalia: The jingle dress has rows of metal cones. Dresses jingle as they move. Modern jingle dresses allow more fluidity. Dancers keep their footwork light, and close to the ground.

Origin: Ojibwe
Story: As the story goes, a young girl was very sick, with no signs of recovering. Her father was very sad. He prayed to the Creator for assistance on what he should do to help his daughter. That night, he had a dream. In this dream the father was shown how to create a dress, and was instructed about a dance that you were to do in the

dress. When he woke up, he set about making the dress and put it on his daughter so that she would dance as he had been instructed to show her. In spite of her illness, she was somehow able to dance, and the more she danced, the stronger she got, and her illness slowly went away (ITC Staff).

Men's Grass: *(Time stamp from video - 0:47)*
The regalia: You can identify the men's grass dance from the fringe on his clothes, representing the grass. Grass dancers also do not wear a bustle. The outfit consists of shirt and pants, with beaded or otherwise decorated belt and side tabs, arm bands, cuffs, and front and back apron, with matching headband and moccasins. Ribbons and fringe are the only mobile parts of his outfit, other than the roach feather (Powwows.com).

Origin: Omaha Tribe of Nebraska
Story: The dominant legend is that a plains boy, born handicapped, yet yearning to dance, was told by his medicine man to seek inspiration in the prairie. Upon doing so, the boy had a vision of himself dancing in the style of the swaying grasses; he returned to his village, shared his vision, and eventually was given back the use of his legs through the first-ever grass dance (ITC Staff).

Men's Traditional: *(Time stamp from video - 1:22)*
The regalia: Men's traditional dancers wear a roach (headdress) made of porcupine hair and deer tail hair. Most dancers wear a shirt, either with or without ribbon decoration. Over the shirt is a breastplate that extends below the waist. They also wear a choker, arm bands, and cuffs. The breach cloth, or apron, can be made of either cloth or leather. Men's traditional dancers wear a feather bustle and is usually u-shaped with a single row of wing or tail feathers and two spikes pointed upward (Powwow.com).

Origin Tribe: Sioux
Origin: The men's traditional dance is a plains Indian style of dance. It embraces their hunting parties, warriors, traditional outfits, their bravery, and courage as people of America who lived off the land long before settlers came. There are two dances that men's traditional dancers should know. One of those dances is called the sneak-up. This is where the dancer kneels to the ground and scouts for enemies' tracks. Then the dancer quickly rises. This symbolizes confrontation with the enemy. In sneak-up songs, dancers should never dance backwards, as it would mean he is retreating from the enemy.

Northern traditional dancers also crow hop. This is a different step from the crow hop women dance. In the crow hop, dancers dip down and then rise up, often swaying their heads from side to side over unmoving shoulders. During the honor, or hard beats, dancers raise their fans or coup sticks to catch the drum's spirit and honor the drum (WeRNative).

Women's Traditional: *(Time stamp from video - 1:52)*
The regalia: You can tell a traditional dancer by her shawl draped over her arm. Northern traditional dancers wear the buckskin, and southern traditional dancers wear a cloth dress.

Origin Tribe: Lakota, Dakota, and Nakota
Origin: The women's traditional dance is the very oldest form of dance for ladies. Females of all ages are seen dancing this very regal and proud style. Pride of heritage, culture, and family can be seen in the faces and demeanor of these well-respected dancers. In fact, when performing this style in competitions, judges watch the ladies to see if the required dignity is retained all throughout the dance.

When moving in the circle, there are northern and southern styles of dancing. Northern style is danced by remaining in one spot, lightly bouncing in rhythm with the drum. Southern style has the women slowly and gracefully walking around the circle in time with the drum, gently stepping toe-heel, toe-heel with the feet appearing to "walk on clouds." Both styles carry a fringed shawl folded over their bent left arm, a purse in their left hand, and a feather fan, usually eagle or hawk in their right hand.

The women hold themselves tall and proud, their bodies straight. The fringe on the shawl is to sway naturally with the movements of the women's feet, not from upper body bending or swinging. The fan is raised in salute when the women hear the drum giving honor beats. Some ladies will also bend at the waist at this time, remaining in one spot or taking a certain number of steps inward toward the middle of the circle. At all times, the dancers are to stay in time with the drum and stop precisely when the drumming ends. The ladies wear knee-length beaded moccasins, leggings, and either a buckskin or cloth dress that has long, open sleeves. There are two styles of buckskin dress; once again northern and southern. The northern style is to completely beaded on the shoulder or cape part of the dress, whereas, the southern style uses beadwork mainly as an accent. Also in buckskin regalia the moccasins are either fully beaded (northern) or accent-beaded (southern). Women's traditional dancers themselves are the most lovely of all with their pride and grace on display in their faces and the way they carry themselves (Cook).

Women's Fancy: *(Time stamp from video - 2:30)*
The regalia: You can tell a fancy dancer by the fringed shawl that is draped over their shoulders, flared skirt, and yoke or vest.

Story: The women's fancy dance is relatively new to the powwow scene. There are a lot of stories about how the fancy dance represents a butterfly. It was the 1920s when the men created the men's fancy. The women created a similar dance, however, it didn't take off until the 1950s. The fancy shawl dance was called the "graceful shawl dance" when it emerged in the 1950s (Whitefield-Madrano).

During the dance's beginning, dancers take smaller steps, close to the ground. The dance today is very athletic. Women spin, kick, and jump all while being light on their feet. Their arms are also extended to showcase the shawl.

Men's Fancy Dance: *(Time stamp from video - 3:05)*
The regalia: Men's fancy dancers usually have two bustles on their back, and they wear a roach (headdress), and carry spinners.

Origin Tribe: Ponca
Origin of dance: The men's fancy dance is a colorful, athletic performance. In the 1920s, Canada and the U.S. government outlawed Native American religious dances, forcing tribes to take their dances underground, and to create new dances that could legally be danced in public. This is how the fancy dance was born.

The fancy dance is attributed to two young Ponca boys who created a fast-moving, audience-pleasing routine in 1928 at the tribe's dance arena in White Eagle, Oklahoma. This was right around the time the intertribal powwow circuit was spreading across the Southern Plains. As other tribes adopted the fancy dance, the moves became increasingly adventurous: cartwheels, splits and back flips. Today, the men's fancy dance is among the most popular events held at a powwow, and has turned into a fierce competition (ITC Staff).

Men & Women's Hoop Dance: *(Time stamp from video - 4:16)*
The regalia: Male hoop dancers will typically wear their breech cloths and ribbon shirt, and female dancers will wear their individual style of dress. Regalia may vary depending on what the dancers prefers to wear.

Origin Tribe: Taos Pueblo
Origin Story: Originally this dance was a men's dance. It was used to tell the story of the creation, and dancers only used 5 hoops. However, the dance has evolved into something that women have been allowed to do. Dancers use

anywhere from 1 to 30 hoops at one time, weaving them through their body making different formations of birds, plants, and animals. Some like to say they are telling the story of the Eagle. The eagle is sacred to Native Americans. A long time ago, when the earth was new, the people were wicked. They fought with each other, and they did not respect the land the Creator had given them. After many warnings, the Creator decided that he was going to destroy the Earth. In a panic the people sent the Eagle to plead with Creator. They knew that the Eagle could fly the highest of all the birds and could reach the Heavens. So the Eagle carried the prayers of the people on his back and was able to convince the Creator to give the people another chance. Today the Eagle feathers are worn and given when we dance. They are used as a reminder, and as a form of prayer. When we dance we are sending our prayers through Eagle to our ancestors. The hoop dance tells the story of the Eagle. As it soars high in the sky it can see every living thing around him. And as the dancer dances the hoop dance, he makes the formations of animals and plants the Eagle sees as it soars (Schramm).

Regalia

Do you remember what Native Americans call what they wear when they dance? **Regalia.** Did you notice in the video that none of the dancers were wearing the same thing? That is because you can't buy regalia at the store. Each one is hand-made. Each one has a different design that represents who the dancer is. Some of the designs may come from their tribe, some designs may come from their clan (a **clan** is a family group within the tribe), and some designs are just because it's their favorite animal or color. But each one is special for that dancer. It takes a lot of hard work to design regalia.

Some dancers begin to dance when they are little babies. Some dancers start later, but they all have to decide what dance they want to do.

If you could dance, which one would you do? And what would you put on your regalia that would represent who you are?

Adaptations for younger grades:

Read *Jingle Dancer* listed in the suggested books. Talk about why it was important for her to dance. What are powwows? Why was her jingle dress special to her, and who she was dancing for? Then refer back to the lesson for the origin story. Pick a few more stories about the other dances to tell students.

Assignments:

Color pages: Pick a dance, and then design the regalia. The color pages are just the outline of the regalia. You have to add the designs and colors. Make sure it tells something about who you are. For older students, ask them to write about why they chose the dance and design. What does it say about who they are?

Take the time to have a few kids come up and describe what they drew, and why it was important to them.

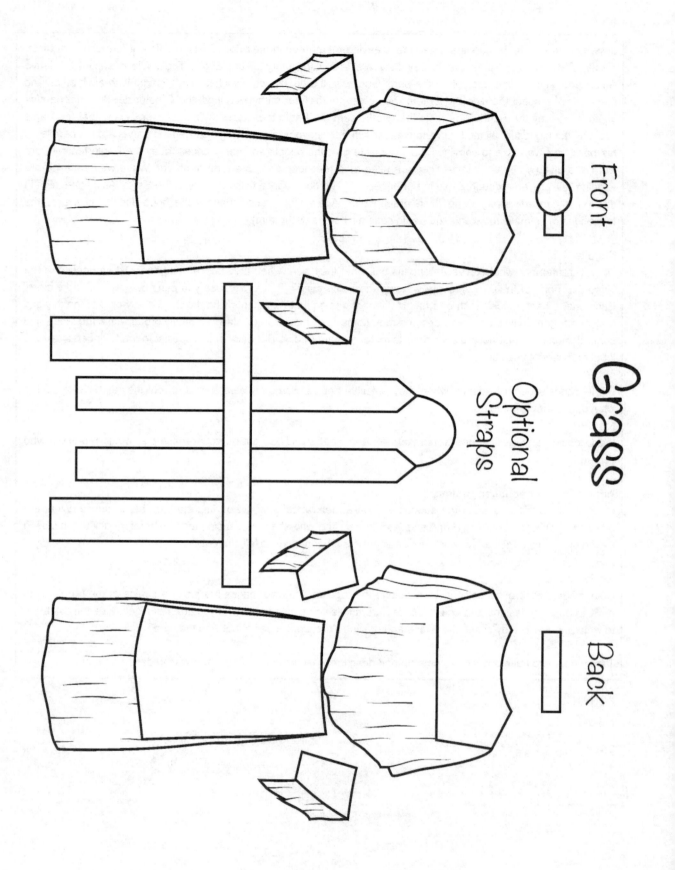

Front

Grass

Optional
Straps

Back

79

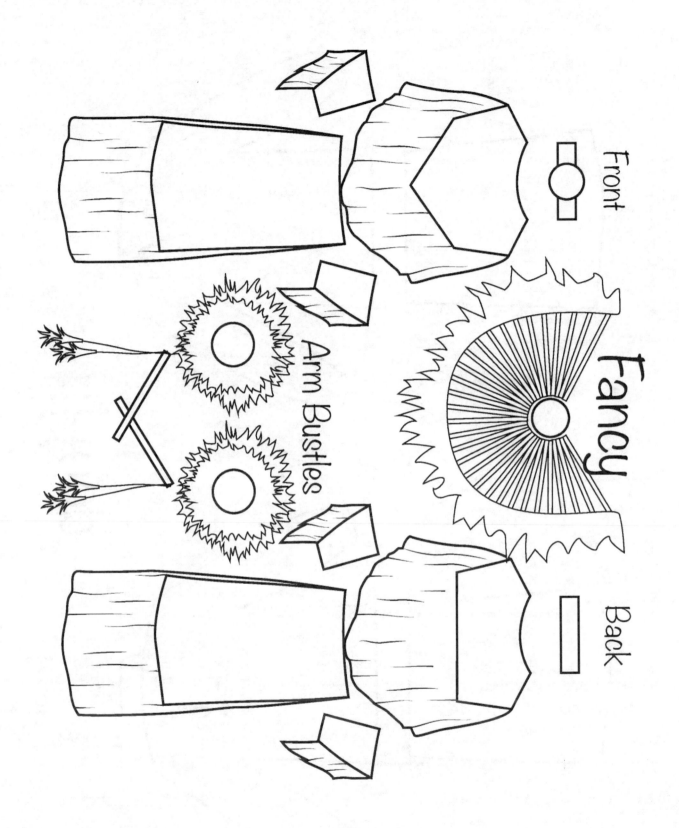

Front

Fancy

Back

Arm Bustles

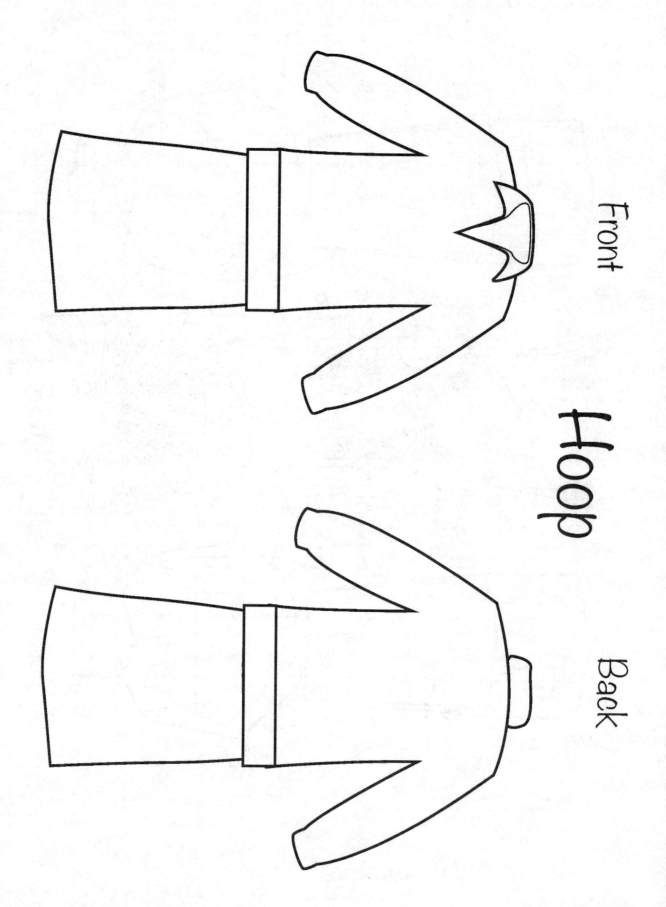

Front

Hoop

Back

81

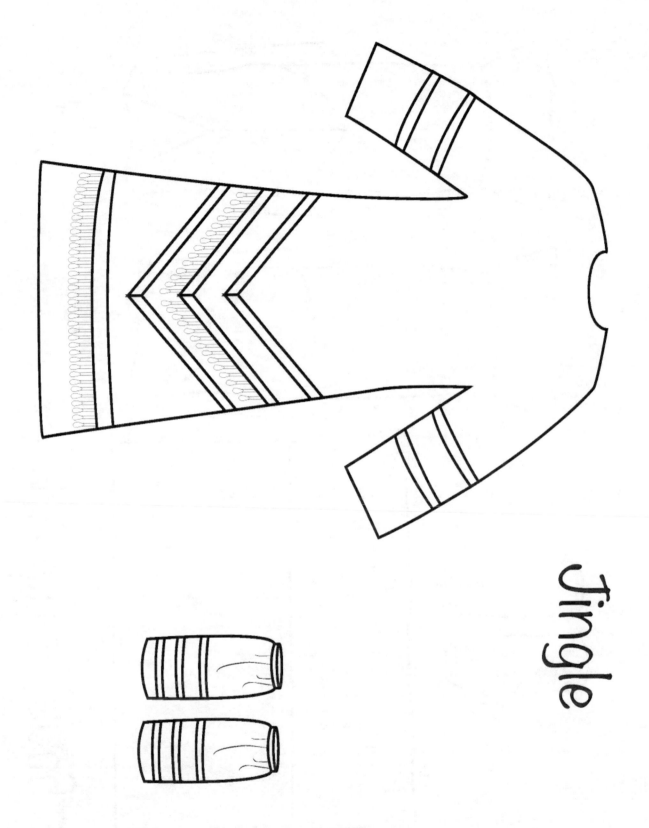

Jingle

Front

Back

Women's Fancy

Women's Hoop

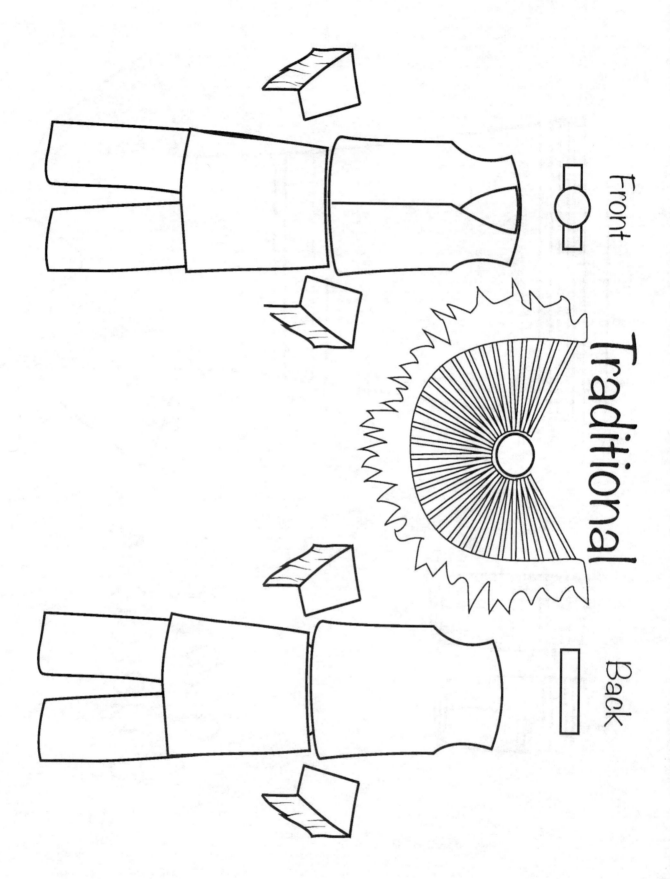

Front

Traditional

Back

85

15.
Lesson 12: Drumming & Song

Lesson: Drumming & Song
Standards:
NCSS: Theme 1
CCSS: Listening & Speaking
2. Integrate and evaluate information presented in diverse media and formats, including visually, quantitatively, and orally.
CCSS: Writing
Gather relevant information from multiple print and digital sources, assess the credibility and accuracy of each source, and integrate the information while avoiding plagiarism.
CCSS Reading
7. Integrate and evaluate content presented in diverse media and formats, including visually and quantitatively, as well as in words.
Utah
Standard 4.M.P.7: Perform and identify rhythm patterns in two-, three-, and four-beat meters using body percussion, voice and simple instruments.

Materials: Hand drum (or something that can make a beat).
Suggested Book: Cherrington, Janelle. *The Drum Beats On.*
Time: 30-60 minutes, depending on grade

Desired Outcomes

Learning Goals:
- I can understand the difference between the different styles of songs, and drum.

Understandings:	Essential Questions:
Students will understand that the drum is important to the Native American culture because the drum represents the heartbeat of the earth. When it is used, we are acknowledging that our Earth is alive and well. The different beats of the drum help dancers know which style to dance, and by listening for the different parts of each push-up dancers can tell when the song will be done.	What is a drum? Why are drums and songs important for Native American culture? Are the people really singing words? What are the different parts to the song? Is there a way to differentiate the songs?

Students will know… (Knowledge & Vocab)	Students will be able to… (Skills)
Drum: A musical instrument. **Push-ups**: Push-ups in a Native song are equivalent to a verse. It is composed of a lead, a body, and honor beats. **Grand Entry**: The song that brings dancers into the dance arena. **Flag Song**: The flag song is similar to a national anthem. **Veterans Song**: A song to honor those that served in war or in civic service. **Sneak up**: A men's dance. It is a dance that tells a story. **Intertribal**: Mean all tribes participate. Intertribal songs refer to social dances. **Crow Hop, Double Beat, Side Step**: Styles of dance that can be differentiated by the different beat of the drum. **Round Dance**: A winter social singing ceremony using hand drums. **Duck and Dive**: Refers to a dance that retells the story of battles between tribes and the U.S. Army.	• Utilize rhythm skills • Utilize reading comprehension skills • Utilize listening, recall, and application skills • Utilize writing skills • Utilize research skills • Apply information learned to another tribe/situation

Evidence of Learning

Performance Tasks:	Success Criteria:
Rhythm activities with class Native American drumming and songs essay and questions **Unit Project Assignment:** Research how to say "Hello," "Goodbye," and "I love you" in your tribe's language.	• I am able to follow directions and listen for the different beats by the teacher and will be able to keep the beat with their feet (walking). • I am able to read the essay and use text evidence.

Learning Plan

The outline is meant to give you background information, and meant to guide you as a teacher. Depending on what grade you teach, you may not go into detail about everything presented. It is good information to have if there are questions. Use the information to give a description of the drums and songs. If you have a hand drum to show the kids, so they can see, bring it and let them try to hit the drum a few times to hear the sound.

Why is this an important topic? We have all seen the movies and TV shows where Natives are dancing and whooping around a fire. While the Natives are dancing, you hear the stereotypical BOOM boom boom boom BOOM boom boom boom BOOM boom in the background. Do you think these songs accurately represent Native American tribes?

What is a drum? A drum is a musical instrument used by a number of different tribes in North America. It is a percussion instrument and is hit to make sounds. It may be struck with a stick or hands depending on where a tribe is located. Traditionally, a drum is made out of a hollow wood body or shell, and the ends covered with stretched animal rawhide (Jansen).

Drums are believed by most Natives to be the heartbeat of our Earth. When they are used, it is an acknowledgment that our Earth is alive and well. The parts of a drum, the wood and animal skin, are said to remain alive in the drum when it is used. Someone outside of the Native American culture might think the wood used is now dead, and the animal skin that is used is from a dead animal, but to Native Americans the tree and the animal remain alive when the drum is used and we can hear its voice (Jansen).

The song structure: When you actually stop and listen to the songs, and the different beats, you realize how complex and beautiful each song is. Every song will have push-ups, which are equivalent to a verse. Contest songs normally have four push-ups and intertribal songs will have six push-ups. A push-up is composed of a LEAD, a BODY, and HONOR BEATS. Each push-up is started with a single singer. He will sing a LEAD to indicate to the other singers around the drum what song is being sung. The BODY of the song has two parts. These parts are separated by a slight pause in northern songs, or by three hard beats in southern songs. The HARD BEATS are sometimes called honor beats. In northern songs, these beats come at the end of each push-up. In southern songs, the honor beats divide the two parts of the body of the song (Jansen).

The drummers and singers at the powwow provide the music for the dancers to move in cultural celebration. Songs consist of key phrases which are repeated. These phrases may be composed of words or syllables (called vocables), which echo the beat of the drum. There are two basic singing styles: northern or southern. In the northern songs, singers maintain a higher pitch, and the southern songs will keep a lower key (The Nanticoke Indian Tribe).

Different Songs:
- Grand Entry: This is a song that brings in the dancers to the dance arena. It is upbeat and lively. This song is usually sung by a drum group hired by the powwow committee to sing appropriate songs for the

entirety of the powwow. During Grand Entry, everyone in the arena is asked to stand as the flags are brought in. First, the flags are carried in which may include the U.S. flag, tribal flags, POW flag, and eagle staffs of various tribes. All of the flags are carried in by veterans. Natives hold the U.S. flag in an honored position. The flag has a dual meaning. First, it is a way to remember all of the ancestors that fought against this country. It also symbolizes the country which Natives are now a part of, and reminds people of the Natives who fought for this country. Important guests of the powwow follow the veterans, the men dancers are next, then the women dancers (Great Mohican Powwow).

- Flag Song: A flag song is comparable to a national anthem (Berry). It is sung in recognition of those that served their people in wars or civic service, including veterans and tribal leaders.

- Victory Song: The victory song is also referred to as a veterans song.

- Sneak Up: Sneak up songs are for male traditional dancers. They normally begin with a ruffle of drumsticks hitting the top of the drum, almost sounding like rolling thunder. The Sneak-Up Dance is an ancient storytelling dance having several origins that became known as a Sneak Up Dance when it was performed in the Wild West Shows of the 1800s. Today, however, it is sometimes still used in the traditional way. The original Lakota Sneak-Up Song, and other more modern sneak-up songs that have been composed, are mainly used as contest songs for Men's Northern Traditional dance contests (Pow-wow.org).

- Intertribal: These songs are social dances. They are sung usually between contest categories. This is a time when everyone is welcome to come into the area and dance his or her style. You do not need to be dressed in dance regalia to dance these dances.

- Crow Hop and Double Beat: The crow hop originated from the Western Tribes. It is meant to mimic the crow as he bounces around the field. One legend states that the crow brought fire to our land to help keep our ancestors alive through the cold winter (The Nanticoke Indian Tribe).

- Round Dance: The Round Dance is one of the most popular social dances. The Round Dance is a circle dance derived from earlier friendship dances. Today everyone is invited to participate whether you are in regalia or not (The Nanticoke Indian Tribe).

- Duck and Dive: Both the Crow people and the Nez Perce have origin stories for this style of song. Both reenact different battles between their tribes and the U.S. army. There are a series of hard beats, but on certain hard beats the dancers duck down as they dance. These beats that require dancers to bend down represent canon fire. In the battles with the U.S. army, warriors would go out into the open to get the army to fire their cannons. When the cannons were fired, the dancers would hide. This was done to get the army to use all of its ammunition for the canon (Ellwood).

Adaptations for younger grades:
Read the book *The Drum Beats* to teach about the importance of the drum, why it is sacred, and where it is used.

Assignments:
At the end of the discussion, tie in the regalia and dance lesson. **Please do not teach any dances**, but tell them that dancers use the beat of the drum to dance. Every time the drumstick hits the drum, dancers are supposed to touch their foot to the ground. So if the drummer is drumming slowly, the dancers dance slowly. Similarly, if the drummer is drumming quickly, then the dancers are expected to dance quickly and keep the same beat as the drum.

Here are a few activities that can coordinate with PE or music. It will help students understand how to follow the beat. **This is not meant to teach a dance, but rhythm.**

Walk in place: With your drum or other instrument, have the kids walk in place and gradually get faster and faster. Make sure students are listening to the beat and following it with their feet. If this is hard, you may want to start with clapping, and then move on to using their feet.

Snake: Have the kids follow the leader in a snake formation, following the beat. The leader gets to weave in and out of desks and around the room. Students can take turns being the leader. Make sure the students are focusing on keeping the beat of the drum as they are moving.

Freeze: When dancers are competing at powwows, they need to listen to the music to know when to stop. Once the drumming stops, they have to stop. Have the kids walking or running in place as they are listening to you drum. They need to listen very carefully, so when you stop drumming, they have to freeze.

Musical Chairs: This is another activity to help kids listen to the music, while keeping the beat. Put chairs in a circle formation. There should be one less chair than students. Students can walk around the chairs keeping the beat of the drum. When the drumming stops, they need to stop and find a chair to sit on. Leaving one child without a chair. The child who is out stands on the side practicing the beat while the others continue. Remember to take a chair out at the end of each round. This is replayed until there is only one student remaining.

16.
Lesson 13: Doctrine of Discovery

Lesson: Doctrine of Discovery
Standards: NCSS: Theme 5 NCSS: Theme 6 CCSS: Listening & Speaking 2. Integrate and evaluate information presented in diverse media & formats, including visually, quantitatively, & orally. CCSS: Writing 2. Write informative/explanatory texts to examine and convey complex ideas and information clearly and accurately through the effective selection, organization, and analysis of content. 7. Conduct short as well as more sustained research projects based on focused questions, demonstrating understanding of the subject under investigation. 8. Gather relevant information from multiple print and digital sources, assess the credibility and accuracy of each source, and integrate the information while avoiding plagiarism. CCSS Reading 7. Integrate and evaluate content presented in diverse media and formats, including visually and quantitatively, as well as in words.
Time: 30-60 minutes, depending on grade level

Desired Outcomes

Learning Goals: • I can explain the concept of the Doctrine of Discovery and the three court cases that make up the Marshall Trilogy.

Understandings: Students will understand the concept of the Doctrine of Discovery and how it affected Native tribes. Students will understand the three court cases that make up the Marshall Trilogy, and their outcomes. They will understand how these court cases make up the framework for Indian law today.	**Essential Questions:** What is the Doctrine of Discovery? What court cases created the framework for Indian law today? What did the Marshall Trilogy establish as far as how it affects Native Americans today?
Students will know… (Knowledge & Vocab) Doctrine of Discovery was the belief held by Christian countries to travel to other lands undiscovered by other Christian countries to "civilize" and exercise dominion over the peoples of the non-Christian country. The "Indian Problem" initiated the framework for the Marshall Trilogy. The Marshall Trilogy is a series of three court cases written by former Supreme Court Chief Justice John Marshall. -*Johnson v. M'Intosh* found that title to lands were tied directly to the US. -*Cherokee Nation v. Georgia* presented a jurisdictional issue and raised the question of what type of relationship Indian nations have with the federal government. -*Worcester v. Georgia* declared only the federal government has rights and authorities over Indian nations. The Marshall Trilogy provides framework for understanding Indian law: 1. The U.S. government has a duty to protect Indian Nations. 2. They have plenary power over Indian nations (meaning they can do whatever they see fit with Indian nations as long as it was exercised in "good faith" and in the "best interest" of the	**Students will be able to… (Skills)** • Utilize summarizing skills • Utilize reading comprehension skills • Utilize listening, recall, and application skills • Utilize writing skills • Utilize research skills • Apply information learned to another tribe/situation

Native people.	

Evidence of Learning

Performance Tasks:	**Success Criteria:**
Doctrine of Discovery worksheet	• Explain the concept of the Doctrine of Discovery.
Unit Project Assignment: Write report/essay on how these events/dates affect Native lives today. Use timeline worksheet.	• List the three court cases in the Marshall Trilogy.
	• Explain how the court cases affect Natives today.

Learning Plan

Lesson: *Essay was written by Alexis Zendejas J.D., a member of the Omaha Tribe of Nebraska and graduate of the James E. Rogers College of Law at the University of Arizona.*

The Legal Origins of Indian Country

The intricacies and boundaries of Indian Country are not organic. They are comprised of hundreds of years of Indian policies and experiments conducted by the United States federal government—and before that monarchies and even religious leaders.

Christendom was on a mission to disseminate their doctrine amongst the heathens. The crusades, the Spanish Inquisition, and many other times in history have demonstrated this mission. Religious leaders declared it a divine right to colonize, civilize, and Christianize the ungodly wherever they may be. From this ecclesiastical edict monarchies found a basis on which to "discover" new non-Christian lands. This basis is known as the Doctrine of Discovery, the right of Christian countries to travel to other lands undiscovered by any other Christian country to "civilize" and exercise dominion over the peoples of the non-Christian country. After the colonization of America, the British monarch promulgated the Proclamation of 1763 that centralized relations with Indian Nations. Relations, contracts, promises, deals, etc. could no longer be individualized. Previous to this Proclamation, colonists would make deals with Indian Nations. By centralizing relations between Indian tribes and the government, the government in effect recognized that Indian Tribes are, at the very least, entities that can make agreements, or at the most, sovereign governments.

After American Independence, relations with Native American tribes became stilted and contentious. The young country attempted to keep centralized relations, but this proved difficult and confusing for states and individual citizens. No one really knew what to do with the Indians. This "Indian Problem" initiated the framework in the Marshall Trilogy. It is a series of three cases written by former Supreme Court Chief Justice John Marshall that laid the framework for Indian law today.

Foundations: The Marshall Trilogy

The first case in the trilogy, *Johnson v. M'Intosh*, gives origin to Indian Title. Chief Justice Marshall found that title to the lands were tied directly to the United States. The reasoning behind the Court's decision was Great Britain gained full title to the lands through the Doctrine of Discovery. "The principle was the discovery game title to the government by whose subjects, or by whose authority, it was made, against all other European governments, which title might be consummated by possession." The Indian tribes as original occupants, and by the permission of the discoverer, only have a right of occupancy. They do not have the full bundle of property rights—they can physically possess and use the land—but the government that discovered them has those rights. The American Revolution and transfer of power between governments shifted those rights from Great Britain to the United States through conquest. This diminished the full bundle of rights that Indians had before European contact and established Aboriginal Title, or Indian Title, reduction the rights to solely a right to inhabit area that Indians inhabited at the point of contact. "…But their rights to complete sovereignty, as independent nations, were necessarily diminished, and their power to dispose of the soil at their own will, to whomsoever they pleased, was denied by the original fundamental principle, that discovery gave exclusive title to those who made it." Indian Title is still an active principle and those tribes that have Indian Title to lands are within the boundaries of "Indian Country," as it pertains to statute.

The second installment in the Marshall Trilogy is *Cherokee Nation v. Georgia*. This case presented a jurisdictional issue and raised the question of what type of relationship Indian Nations have with the federal government. The Supreme Court Justices were split 2-2-2, each opinion classifying Indian Tribes in a different way. One opinion was that the text of the Constitution classified Indian Tribes as independent sovereigns creating an international relationship between Indian Tribes and the United States. Another opinion thought that tribes were wholly under the jurisdiction of the federal and state governments. The majority opinion of the Court ruled that tribes were not foreign nations. The Court decided that Indian Nations were "domestic dependent nations" existing as wards of the federal government. The Court explained that because, "[t]hey occupy a territory to which we assert a title independent of their will… [and] they are in a state of pupilage. Their relation to the United States resembles that of a ward to his guardian." The court goes on to describe the essence of a trust relationship corresponding to Indian Nation's new status asserting that, "being so under the sovereignty and dominion of the United States, that any attempt to acquire their lands, or to form a political connection with them, would be considered by all as an invasion of our territory, and an act of hostility."

The Court also used a textual argument with language from the Constitution. The commerce clause gives Congress the power to, "regulate commerce with foreign nations, and among the several states, **and** with the Indian tribes" (emphasis added). The word "and" gave textual support to the Court's argument that tribes were not foreign nations because the authors of the Constitution would not have had to differentiate between foreign nations and tribes had they meant for tribes to be classified as foreign nations. Marshall opined, "[i]n this clause they are as clearly contradistinguished by a name appropriate to themselves, from foreign nations, as from the several states composing the union." This case announced that Indian Tribe are wards to the federal government conferring upon the United States a duty to protect and thereby giving the United States further right to insert themselves in proprietary affairs of the Indian Tribes and Indian Country.

The last case in the trilogy, *Worcester v. Georgia*, declared only the federal government has the rights and authorities over Indian Nations. Marshall stated in his opinion that, "[t]he treaties and laws of the United States contemplate the Indian territory as completely separated from that of the states; and provided that all intercourse with them shall be carried on exclusively by the government of the union." Rights and jurisdictions do not extend to the states regardless of where the Indian Nations reside. The United States exercised the principle of preemption by stating that the laws of the states have "not force" on Indian Nations. The United States Constitution and the Bill of Rights put a limiting power on states' authority as well as tribal inherent sovereignty.

The Marshall Trilogy proves the basic framework for understanding Indian Law at its core. These cases outline that the federal government has (1) a duty to protect Indian Nations—while Indians have inherent sovereignty they are subject to federal authority and (2) the federal government has plenary power over Indian Nations—meaning they can do whatever they see fit with or to the Indian Nations as long as it was exercised in "good faith" and in the "best interest" of the tribes. These points play out in the reasoning for how the rest of Indian Country came to be.

Discussion: Looking back at the past lessons, how does the Doctrine of Discovery affect Native Americans today?

Assignments:
Have students fill out worksheet as you talk about the Doctrine of Discovery and the court cases behind the Marshall Trilogy.

Name: _____ Date: _____

Doctrine of Discovery

1. Summarize the Doctrine of Discovery.

2. Name the three court cases that make up the Marshall Trilogy, and summarize what they talk about:

   a.

   b.

   c.

3. How does the Doctrine of Discovery impact Native Americans today?

17.
Sources

The list of resources below are ones that I used to help write the lesson plans or that I thought you would find useful as a teaching tool. But remember, your most important resource is the Native families you have in your school. Let them be a part of the learning for you and for your class!

Community:
1. Your local Title VI, American Indian/Alaskan Native Education Program. The Title VI program is a federally funded grant program that most school districts have. These programs will often offer tutoring or cultural activities for the Native families in the district. If you do not know if your district has one, call the district offices. They will be able to direct you to the right people.

Videos:
1. *Running Brave*. Directed by D.S. Everett, Englander Productions, 1983.
2. *Unspoken: America's Native American Boarding Schools*. KUED, https://video.kued.org/video/unspoken-americas-native-american-boarding-schools-oobt1r/
3. *We Shall Remain: A Native History of Utah*, 5 Volumes (Paiute, Ute, Navajo, Goshute, Northwestern Shoshone). Produced by John Howe, KUED, https://www.kued.org/whatson/we-shall-remain-native-history-america-and-utah, 2016.
4. *The Long Walk: Tears of the Navajo*. Produced by John Howe, KUED, https://www.kued.org/whatson/the-long-walk-tears-the-navajo, 2007.
5. *Healing the Warrior's Heart*. Produced by Taki Telonidis, Gary Robinson of Tribal Eye Productions, KUED, 2014.
6. *Medicine Woman*. Directed by Christine Lesiak, produced by Christine Lesiak, Princella RedCorn, www.pbs.org/video/medicine-woman-full-episode, 2016.
7. *Battle Over Bears Ears*. Produced by Nancy Green, KUED, https://www.kued.org/whatson/kued-productions/battle-over-bears-ears, 2018.

Websites:
American Indians in Children's Literature (AICL) , https://americanindiansinchildrensliterature.blogspot.com Established in 2006, American Indians in Children's Literature (AICL) provides critical perspectives and analysis of indigenous peoples in children's and young adult books, the school curriculum, popular culture, and society.

Online Sources:
"About." *Eighth Generation*, https://eighthgeneration.com/pages/about-us. Accessed 22 May 2018.
American Indian Education Fund. "Notable Native Americans: Ben Nighthorse Campbell." http://www.nativepartnership.org/site/PageServer?pagename=aief_hist_nna_bencampbell. Accessed 22 May 2018.
American Indian Education Fund. "Notable Native Americans: John Bennet Herrington." http://www.nativepartnership.org/site/PageServer?pagename=aief_hist_nna_johnherrington. Accessed 22 May 2018.
American Indian Movement. "The Indian Termination Policy." https://americanindianmovementehs.weebly.com/indian-termination-policy.html. Accessed 12 March 2019.
American Indian Relief Council. "History and Culture: Boarding Schools." http://www.nativepartnership.org/site/PageServer?pagename=airc_hist_boardingschools. Accessed 22 May 2018.
Ankeny, Jason. "Robbie Robertson." *Biography*. http://theband.hiof.no/band_members/robbie.html. Accessed 22 May 2018.
Berry, Carol. "The True Language of a Powwow Drum." *Indian Country Today*, 10 March 2011, https://newsmaven.io/indiancountrytoday/archive/the-true-language-of-a-pow-wow-drum-EyVawaQ9vUq1HqXvyIKfNw/. Accessed 16 June 2018.

"Bronson Koening." *Wisconsin Men's Basketball*, http://uwbadgers.com/roster.aspx?rp_id=150. Accessed 22 May 2018.

Bush, George W. The White House. "Remarks by the President in a Ceremony Honoring the Navajo Code Talkers." *The White House*, 26 July 2001, https://georgewbush-whitehouse.archives.gov/news/releases/2001/07/20010726-5.htmlhttps://georgewbush-whitehouse.archives.gov/news/release/2001/07/20010726-5.html. Accessed 1 April 2018.

Central Intelligence Agency. "Navajo Code Talkers and the Unbreakable Code." 6 Nov. 2018, https://www.cia.gov/news-information/featured-story-archive/2008-featured-story-archive/navajo-code-talkers/. Accessed 22 May 2018.

Changing the Face of Medicine. "Dr. Lori Arviso Alvord." https://cfmedicine.nlm.nih.gov/physicians/biography_7.html. Accessed 22 May 2018.

National Museum of the American Indian. "Code Talking." www.nmai.si.edu/education/codetalkers/html/chapter4.html. Accessed 22 May 2018.

Cook, Roy. "Women Dance Styles." *Soaring Eagle Sentinel,* http://soaringeagles.americanindiansource.com/sentinel/Women_Dance_Styles.html. Accessed 22 May 2018.

"Cory Witherill | Native American." *Defining Cultures,* https://www.definingcultures.com/cory-witherill-native-american/. Accessed 22 May 2018.

"Deb Haaland, Democrat for Congress." https://debforcongress.com/about-deb. Accessed 22 May 2019.

Ellwood, Lisa J. Indian Country Today. "Two Shots From That Cannon: The History and Significance of the Duck and Dive." *Indian Country Today*, 9 April 2016, https://newsmaven.io/indiancountrytoday/archive/two-shots-from-that-cannon-the-history-and-significance-of-the-duck-and-dive-pFPFSb70x0OyPc4G1W2NgA/. Accessed 16 June 2018.

Federal Recognition Services by American Ancestors. "7 Criteria for Federal Recognition." http://www.federalrecognition.com/services-2/. Accessed 22 May 2018.

G., Paul.Powwows.com. "Grass Dancing." *Powwows.com*, 21 July 2011, http://www.powwows.com/grass-dancing/. Accessed 1 May 2018.

G., Paul. "Northern Traditional Dancing." *Powwow.com*, 21 July 2011, http://www.powwows.com/northern-traditional-dancing/. Accessed 16 June 2018.

"General Authorities and General Officers: Elder Larry J. Echo Hawk." *The Church of Jesus Christ of Latter-day Saints*, https://www.lds.org/church/leader/larry-echo-hawk?lang=eng. Accessed 22 May 2018.

"Get to Know the Thompson Brothers." *Nike News*, 20 July 2015, https://news.nike.com/news/thompson-brothers-lacrosse. Accessed 22 May 2016.

Golshan, Tara. "Paulette Jordan, running to be the first Native American governor, wins Idaho's Democratic primary." *Vox*, 16 May 2018, https://www.vox.com/2018/5/16/17357906/idaho-governor-results-paulette-jordan-democratic-primary. Accessed 16 June 2018.

Granados, Tino. "#IAMNOTACOSTUME." *Urban Native Era,* 5 Oct. 2017, http://www.urbannativeera.com/2017/10/05/1/. Accessed 19 June 2018.

Great Mohican Pow-Wow. "What is a Pow Wow." http://www.mohicanpowwow.com/what-is-a-pow-wow.php. Accessed 6 May 2018.

"Indian Child Welfare Act (ICWA)." *U.S. Department of the Interior Indian Affairs,* https://www.bia.gov/bia/ois/dhs/icwa. Accessed 01 April 2018.

ITC Staff. "Origins of the Grass Dance." *Indian Country Today*, 6 April 2011, https://indiancountrymedianetwork.com/news/origins-of-the-grass-dance/. Accessed 16 June 2018.

ICT Staff. "Origins of Women's Jingle Dress Dancing." *Indian Country Today*, 28 Jan. 2011, https://indiancountrymedianetwork.com/news/origins-of-womens-jingle-dress-dancing/. Accessed 1 April 2018.

"Iroquois Confederacy." *War Paths 2 Peace Pipes,* https://www.warpaths2peacepipes.com/native-american-indians/iroquois-confederacy.htm. Accessed 20 April 2018.

Jiang, Caroline et al., "Racial and Gender Disparities in Suicide Among Young Adults Aged 18-24: United States, 2009-2013." *Health E-Stats*, September 2015, https://www.cdc.gov/nchs/data/hestat/suicide/racial_and_gender_2009_2013.htmhttps://www.cdc.gov/nchs/data/hest at/suicide/racial_and_gender_2009_2013.htm. Accessed 16 June 2018.

Lajimodiere, Denise K. "Native American Boarding Schools." *MNOpedia*, 7 June 2016, http://www.mnopedia.org/native-american-boarding-schools. Accessed 01 May 2018.

Manatake American Indian Council. "Tribes Forced to Prove Existence." https://www.manataka.org/page240.html. Accessed 11 March 2019.

"Maria Tallchief Biography." *Encyclopedia of World Biography*, http://www.notablebiographies.com/St-Tr/Tallchief-Maria.html. Accessed 22 May 2018.

"Men's Northern Traditional." *WeRNative*, https://www.wernative.org/articles/men-39-s-northern-traditional. Accessed 01 April 2018.

National Museum of the American Indian. "Boarding Schools." http://www.nmai.si.edu/education/codetalkers/html/chapter3.html. Accessed 01 April 2018.

NDN Sports Staff. "Ashton Loclear (Lumbee) Set to Compete in Women's Qualification Round at 2017 World Championships Today." *NDNSports.com*, 4 Oct. 2017, http://www.ndnsports.com/ashton-locklear-lumbee-set-to-compete-in-womens-qualification-round-at-2017-world-cha mpionships-today/. Accessed 22 May 2018.

Notah Begay III Foundation. "Notah Begay III Bio." http://www.nb3foundation.org/notah-begay-iii-bio/. Accessed 22 May 2018.

Ravits, Jessica. "The Sacred Land at the Center of the Dakota Pipeline Dispute." *CNN*, 1 Nov. 2016, https://www.cnn.com/2016/11/01/us/standing-rock-sioux-sacred-land-dakota-pipeline/index.html. Accessed 16 June 201801 November 2016.

"Sam Bradford, Football Player." *Famous Birthdays*, https://www.famousbirthdays.com/people/sam-bradford.html. Accessed 22 May 2018.

"Sharice Davids." https://www.shariceforcongress.com/about. Accessed 30 April 2019.

"Shoni Schimmel." *WNBA*, http://www.wnba.com/player/shoni-schimmel/. Accessed 22 May 2018.

"Sneak Up Dance." *Pow-wow.org*, https://www.pow-wow.org/sneak-dance/. Accessed 01 May 2018.

"Suzan Shown Harjo." *Smithsonian*, https://www.si.edu/about/bios/suzan-shown-harjo. Accessed 22 May 2018.

The Nanticoke Indian Tribe. "Native American Dance Styles." http://www.nanticokeindians.org/page/culture. Accessed 01 May 2018.

The Nanticoke Indian Tribe. "What is a Powwow?" http://www.nanticokeindians.org/page/what-powwow. Accessed 01 May 2018.

"Tribal Sovereignty: History and Law." www.nativeamericancaucus.org. Accessed 1 April 2018.

"Adam Beach biography." *tribute.ca*, https://www.tribute.ca/people/adam-beach/5726/. Accessed 22 May 2018.

Tuscarora and Six Nations Website. "The Constitution of the Iroquois Nations." http://tuscaroras.com/index.php?option=com_content&view=article&id=20&Itemid=22. Accessed 18 June 2018.

Utah Diné Bikéyah. http://utahdinebikeyah.org/. Accessed 28 May 2018.

"Wes Studi Biography." *IMDB*, https://www.imdb.com/name/nm0836071/bio. Accessed 22 May 2018.

"What is a Native American Powwow?." *Powwows.com*, http://www.powwows.com/main/native-american-pow-wow/. Accessed 1 May 2018.

Whitefield, Autumn. "The Evolving Beauty of the Fancy Shawl Dance." *Indian Country Today*, 20 Mar. 2011, https://indiancountrymedianetwork.com/news/the-evolving-beauty-of-the-fancy-shawl-dance/. Accessed 16 June 2018.

"World War II." *Encyclopedia Britannica*, https://www.britannica.com/event/World-War-II. Accessed 01 April 2018.

Books/Articles/Other:

Alexie, Sherman. *Thunder Boy Jr.* New York, Hachette Book Group, Inc., 2016.

Begay, Crystal Tewa. "John Brown Jr." 28 February 2018.

Bigelow, Bill & Peterson, Bob. *Rethinking Columbus, The Next 500 Years*. Rethinking Schools, Ltd. Milwaukee, Wisconsin, 1998.

Bunting, Eve. *Cheyenne Again*. New York, Clarion Books, 1995.

Cherrington, Janelle. *The Drum Beats on*. New York, Scholastic Inc., 2002.

Duncan, Violet. *When We Dance*. 2013.

Echo Hawk, Terry. *Call Me Little Echo Hawk*. Springville, Cedar Fort, 2005.

Fletcher, Alice C. & La Flesche, Francis. *The Omaha Tribe Vol. 1*. Lincoln, University of Nebraska Press, 1992.

Hoagland Hunter, Sara. *The Unbreakable Code*. Flagstaff, Rising Moon, 1996.

Jackson, Jake. *Native American Myths*. London, Flame Tree Publishing, 2014.

Jordan-Fenton, Christy & Pokiak-Fenton, Margaret. *When I was Eight*. U.S.A., Annick Press Ltd. 2013.

Jordan-Fenton, Christy & Pokiak-Fenton, Margaret. *Not my Girl*. U.S.A., Annick Press Ltd. 2014.

Littlefield, Holly. *Children of the Boarding Schools*. Minneapolis, Carolrhoda Books Inc., 2001.

ITC Staff. "Men's Fancy Dance." *Indian Country Today*, 2 December 2010.

Jansen, Dustin. Personal interview. 5 November 2016.

Macfarlan, Allan A. *Native American Tales and Legends*. Mineola, Dover Publications, Inc., 1968.

McGhee, Robert. *State of the Native Youth Report*. 2016.

National Congress of American Indians. *An Introduction to Indian Nations in the United States*, 2003, pp. 3. Accessed 02 February 2018.

Palmer, Merry M. *The Creator and Coyote: A Ute Mountain Ute Tale*. San Juan School District Media Center, 2006.

"Billy Mills: The Path to the Medal." Running Strong for American Indian Youth, 2016

Sheinkin, Steve. *Undefeated: Jim Thorpe and the Carlisle Indian School Football Team*. New York, Roaring Books Press, 2017.

Schramm, Meredith. Personal experience. 10 April 2018.

Smith, Cynthia Leitich. *Jingle Dancer*. New York, Morrow Junior Books, 2000.

Zendejas, Alexis. "The Legal Origins of Indian Country." University of Arizona, 2018.

Zendejas, Edouardo. *Mascots That Honor Indians: The Audacity of a Dope for Suggesting Schools Change Their Indian Mascots*, Honor Indians Institute, 2009.

About the Author

Meredith Schramm is an enrolled member of the Omaha Tribe of Nebraska. She graduated from Brigham Young University (BYU) in 2005 with a Bachelor of Science in exercise science, with an emphasis in public school teaching. Meredith has taught PE since graduating in 2005. She has written curriculum for an independent study program, as well as worked on an accreditation team for two high school therapy programs. Meredith started working with the Indian Education Program for Provo City Schools in 2001 as a tutor while in college. She continues to work with the program in other capacities. Meredith has been married to Benjamin Schramm since 2004. They have 3 daughters and live in Lehi, Utah.
Photo Credit: Annie Smith

About the Illustrator & Cover

Ruben Zendejas is an enrolled member of the Omaha Tribe of Nebraska. He will graduate from Brigham Young University (BYU) in 2019 with a Bachelor of Art in Portuguese with a minor in Nonprofit Management. Ruben plans to attend law school. He was also a member of BYU's performing group, Living Legends. Ruben is married to Shanoah, and lives in Provo, Utah with their son.

We decided on using a ledger art design on the cover for a few reasons. Ledger art is a common form of art medium from the plains tribes. In the 1960s and 1970s, accounting ledger paper was commonly available on reservations. The art form brought old stories to life in a new medium. With these lesson plans, we are trying to tie in old traditions with the new, to show how the past is part of the present, and to demonstrate why both are needed to understand the Native American culture today.
Photo Credit: Heather Clegg

~For my three 'girl-illas' and my amazing husband.

~Special thanks to
Running Strong for American Indian Youth Foundation
&
Provo City School District